# Create an Abundant, Thriving Garden with Ease

Caitlind E. Collins

All rights reserved. Copyright © 2023 Caitlind E. Collins

COPYRIGHT © 2023 Caitlind E. Collins

All rights reserved.

Maintain a reading journal; documenting thoughts and reflections enhances retention and personal growth.

Incorporate lean proteins; they support muscle growth and provide sustained energy.

Your journey is a reflection of your spirit's resilience; embrace each step with gratitude.

Engage in regular cardiovascular check-ups; heart health is foundational to overall well-being.

# Introduction

This book is a comprehensive resource that empowers individuals to create and maintain their own self-sufficient gardens. This guide is designed to help you cultivate a garden that not only provides for your basic food needs but also promotes sustainability and resilience in your everyday life.

The History of the Victory Garden sets the foundation by exploring the historical significance of victory gardens and their role in promoting self-sufficiency during times of crisis. Understanding the origins of victory gardens can inspire and motivate you to embark on your own journey towards self-sufficiency.

Creating Your Survival Victory Garden Step-By-Step takes you through the process of designing and establishing your self-sufficient garden. It provides a step-by-step approach, from selecting the right location and preparing the soil to choosing the appropriate crops and planting strategies. This section guides you in creating a garden that meets your specific needs and maximizes your chances of success.

Starting Your Seeds Step-By-Step focuses on the crucial task of seed starting. It provides detailed instructions on selecting and germinating seeds, as well as caring for seedlings until they are ready to be transplanted. This section equips you with the knowledge and skills to start your plants from scratch, ensuring a healthy and thriving garden.

Crops to Grow in Your Victory Garden offers valuable insights into the types of crops that are well-suited for self-sufficiency and sustainable living. It highlights a variety of vegetables, fruits, and herbs that are nutritious, productive, and easy to grow. This section helps you make informed choices about the crops that best align with your goals and resources.

7 Persistent Produce introduces perennial vegetables that continue to yield crops year after year, providing a sustainable source of food in your garden. It explores a selection of perennial vegetables and offers guidance on growing and maintaining them effectively. By incorporating these perennial crops into your garden, you can enhance its long-term productivity.

How To Grow Crazy Giant Vegetables Naturally takes gardening to the next level by delving into the art of growing oversized and impressive vegetables. It provides tips and techniques for maximizing plant growth and achieving extraordinary results. This section adds an element of fun and excitement to your self-sufficient garden, allowing you to showcase your gardening skills and enjoy the rewards of your efforts.

Unlocking Your Super Soil reveals the secrets to creating nutrient-rich soil that supports healthy plant growth. It covers the importance of soil composition, organic matter, and soil amendments. By understanding the principles of soil fertility, you can optimize the growing conditions in your garden and cultivate bountiful harvests.

A Breakthrough To Bigger & Better Tasting Everything explores innovative techniques and strategies for enhancing the flavor and quality of your homegrown produce. It uncovers methods for maximizing flavor and nutritional value, ensuring that your self-sufficient garden produces not only an abundance of food but also delicious and nourishing crops.

The Amazing Abundant Crop Producer introduces a gardening technique or tool that significantly boosts productivity and crop yields. It provides insights into a specific method or device that can enhance the efficiency and effectiveness of your garden. By incorporating this technique or tool, you can achieve remarkable results and increase your self-sufficiency.

A Victory Garden's Best Friend explores the importance of beneficial insects and pollinators in your garden. It highlights the role of bees, butterflies, and other beneficial creatures in plant pollination and pest control. This section provides guidance on creating a pollinator-friendly garden environment and attracting beneficial insects to support the health and productivity of your crops.

7 Must-Have Medicinal Herbs introduces a selection of medicinal herbs that you can grow in your self-sufficient garden. It explores the health benefits and uses of these herbs, empowering you to cultivate your own natural remedies. By incorporating these medicinal herbs into your garden, you can enhance your self-sufficiency and promote wellness in your daily life.

4 Super Seeds for Sure-Fire Survival focuses on the importance of seed saving and the selection of resilient and adaptable plant varieties. It identifies four key seed varieties that are known for their hardiness and reliability in various growing conditions. This section equips you with the knowledge and skills to save seeds and ensure a sustainable source of future plantings.

Creating Your Water World emphasizes the importance of water conservation and harvesting in a self-sufficient garden. It provides techniques and strategies for collecting and utilizing rainwater, as well as managing irrigation effectively. This section helps you optimize water resources and minimize waste, ensuring the long-term sustainability of your garden.

The Way To Naturally Eliminate Garden Pests explores organic pest control methods and techniques. It offers natural solutions for managing common garden pests without relying on harmful chemicals. This section empowers you to protect your crops from pests while maintaining an eco-friendly and sustainable approach to gardening.

More Pest Control Tips For Your Garden expands on the topic of pest control by providing additional tips and strategies for keeping unwanted pests at bay. It covers a range of preventive measures and organic remedies that can be used to deter pests and maintain the health of your plants. This section equips you with the knowledge to address pest issues effectively and sustainably.

Storing & Hoarding Your Harvest highlights the importance of proper storage and preservation techniques to make the most of your garden's bounty. It offers guidance on storing fruits, vegetables, and herbs to extend their shelf life and maintain their nutritional value. This section ensures that your hard-earned harvest can be enjoyed throughout the year, contributing to your self-sufficiency.

Saving Seeds for Sustainable Gardening focuses on the practice of seed saving as a means of preserving plant diversity and ensuring future harvests. It covers the basics of seed saving, including harvesting, cleaning, and storing seeds for long-term viability. This section empowers you to become self-reliant in seed production and contributes to the sustainability of your garden.

Shooting Fish in a Barrel introduces aquaponics, a sustainable gardening system that combines fish farming with hydroponics. It explains the principles of aquaponics and guides you through the process of setting up your own system. This section expands your self-sufficiency options by incorporating fish production and hydroponic gardening into your overall strategy.

Reasons to Grow Your Own Victory Garden presents compelling reasons for embracing self-sufficiency and cultivating your own victory garden. It explores the benefits of growing your own food, such as increased self-reliance, improved food quality, and reduced environmental impact. This section inspires and motivates you to embark on your self-sufficient gardening journey.

Tower Gardening Questions and Answers offers insights into vertical gardening techniques and the use of tower gardens. It addresses common questions and concerns related to tower gardening, providing practical tips and advice. This section expands your gardening options by exploring vertical space and maximizing your garden's productivity.

Container Victory Gardening focuses on the practice of gardening in containers, making it accessible to individuals with limited space or mobility. It provides guidance on selecting containers, choosing suitable crops, and maintaining container gardens effectively. This section demonstrates how self-sufficient gardening can be adapted to different settings and circumstances.

Edible Landscapes for Survivalists explores the concept of edible landscaping and its potential for self-sufficiency. It encourages the integration of food-producing plants into your landscape, creating a harmonious and productive outdoor environment. This section demonstrates how aesthetics and functionality can be combined to enhance both the beauty and the practicality of your garden.

Permaculture - Path to Long-Term Sustainability & Survival introduces the principles and practices of permaculture as a holistic approach to sustainable living. It explores the integration of ecological design, regenerative agriculture, and community resilience. This section empowers you to embrace a long-term vision of self-sufficiency and engage in practices that restore and regenerate the natural environment.

In conclusion, this is a comprehensive resource that covers a wide range of topics to help you create and maintain a self-sufficient garden. From understanding the history and principles of self-sufficiency to practical techniques for gardening, seed saving, pest control, and more, this guide equips you with the knowledge and skills needed to achieve sustainable and resilient living. Whether you have ample space or limited resources, this guide provides options and strategies to adapt self-sufficiency to your specific circumstances. Embrace the journey towards self-sufficiency and enjoy the rewards of a bountiful and sustainable garden.

# Contents

1. The History of the Victory Garden ................................................................. 1
2. Creating Your Survival Victory Garden Step-By-Step .................................... 4
3. Starting Your Seeds Step-By-Step ................................................................ 27
4. Crops to Grow in Your Victory Garden ......................................................... 43
5. 7 Persistent Produce (Perennial Vegetables That Keep On Giving) ............. 48
6. How To Grow Crazy Giant Vegetables Naturally (Become King Of The Crops) ... 53
7. Unlocking Your Super Soil ............................................................................ 65
8. A Breakthrough To Bigger & Better Tasting Everything ............................... 69
9. The Amazing Abundant Crop Producer ........................................................ 74
10. A Victory Gardens Best Friend ...................................................................... 79
11. 7 Must Have Medicinal Herbs (Natures Doctor in Your Yard) ....................... 86
12. 4 Super Seeds for Sure-Fire Survival ............................................................. 95
13. Creating Your Water World (Harvesting Water So You Can Harvest Your Crops) 102
14. The #1 Way To Naturally Eliminate Garden Pest (When Your Garden Thrives, 106
15. More Pest Control Tips For Your Garden ..................................................... 116
16. Storing & Hoarding Your Harvest (So You Have No Need for the Store) ..... 123
17. Saving Seeds for Sustainable Gardening (Building Your Own Seed ............. 129
18. Shooting Fish in a Barrel (Growing Tilapia in Barrel or IBC Aquaponics) ..... 134
19. Reasons to Grow Your Own Victory Garden ................................................ 140
20. Tower Gardening Questions and Answers ................................................... 144
21. Container Victory Gardening ........................................................................ 151
22. Edible Landscapes For Survivalist ................................................................. 159
23. Permaculture – Path To Long Term Sustainability & Survival ...................... 169

# 1. The History of the Victory Garden

We all know that in states of war, there is always a shortage of food supply. More and more people become hungrier with each passing day as food supply becomes scarcer. This is why victory gardens, also known as war gardens or food gardens for defense were created. These gardens can help alleviate the food shortage and are created in various private and public lands.

Victory gardens were prevalent during World War I and World War II in the US, UK, Canada, and Germany. Additionally, these gardens were not only perceived as a means to aid the pressure on public food supply but also served as a morale booster to the community in the sense that gardeners felt empowered by their contribution to society. Such gardens were actually able to supply about 41% of the country's food supply during the war.

Charles Lathrop Pack was responsible for propagating these gardens. In March of 1917, he, together with the National War Garden Commission, launched the Victory Gardens campaign. During World War I, food supply drastically fell and most European countries experienced dramatic food shortage. Most agriculture laborers were recruited into the military and remaining farm lands were devastated.

Pack conceived the idea that food can actually be grown in non-farm lands, without the use of the manpower that was normally used in agriculture, and without the transportation facilities needed. He then promoted the Victory Gardens campaign which was able to convert available public and private idle lands into more than 5 million gardens, and the value of the food supply exceeded $1.2 billion by the end of the war.

Though there was constant supply of canned goods from the UK, a poster campaign that was launched encouraged even more people to grow their own Victory Gardens that was able to supply about 40% of the country's fruits and vegetables during that time. The campaign encouraged both urban and suburban homes to produce their own vegetables. The effort was said to have helped lower the prices of vegetables in the market and was able to feed the troops that defended the country. The effort helped the government save money on military expenses.

According to some studies, one of the major reasons for the dramatic food shortage during the war was the forced internment of Japanese-Americans. Japanese farmers in California were then responsible for producing 40% of the country's food crops valued at more than $40 million annually. During the war, they were evicted from California and left about 200,000 acres of farmland in California idle.

The parcels of land were then claimed by British immigrants and people from the Dust Bowl region of the US. Since these people were not familiar to the climate in California, they failed to match the production of the Japanese farmers. As a result, there was a significant food shortage and thus, the idea of Victory Gardens was conceived to address the food shortage at the time.

The Victory Gardens were able to help prevent further hunger in the country. Today, there is a mass efforts being done by schools, communities, homesteaders and people from all walks of life looking to restore this campaign and to convert idle public spaces to urban backyards into something more productive, healthy and helpful for the home, the community and the economy.

*Questions:*
Who thought of the Victory Garden campaign?
- Charles Lathrop Pack

What year was the Victory Garden campaign launched?

- 1917

What is one of the major reasons why there was food shortage during the war?
- Japanese-Americans' forced internment

How much percentage of the country's food supply was this campaign able to produce during the war?
- 41%

Why was the Victory Garden campaign launched?
- To augment the country's food supplies.

## 2. Creating Your Survival Victory Garden Step-By-Step

Let's jump right in to creating your own Survivalist Victory Garden.

First thing you want to do is pick a location to turn from free space to food place.

This is the area we selected.

We are not planting this entire space. We are going to create 14 foot rows that are 3 feet wide in a u-shape formation creating a keyhole growing area.

After trying to turn this area with a shovel, it felt like trying to cut bricks with a plastic butter knife. This Texas clay soil is so dry and so hard I had to soften it up first by using a tiller.

As you can see from the picture above, as I took the tiller across the planting areas, even after several runs, the clay is so hard the tiller hasn't done much damage.

But no worries, after taking the clay to task a little longer, it softened up.

With the planting area loosened up, it's time to amend the soil.

Here's what I'm going to use.

We'll be using some pea gravel first to till down further into the clay for better drainage. Also, we will be using compost & manure and landscape growers mix to give more fertility to the soil.

Now if you look in that white bucket you see this…

This is some of the most powerful stuff you will ever put into your ground that will pay you food dividends unlike anything else and the dividends will far outlast multiple lifetimes. Yes… we are talking about an impact today that last for generations.

So what is this stuff?

The white stuff is "Sea Mineral Solids" and the black stuff is "Biochar" and in that clear plastic back is Azomite. Here's another picture so you can see it.

Refer to the chapters on Sea Mineral Solids, Biochar and Azomite later in this book so you can understand why these are so powerful and important to immediately use in your garden.

Moving on, the next thing we want to do is add the pea gravel.

Once the pea gravel is down, I'm going to spread it with a rake and then add the compost & manure mix as shown below.

Once the entire area is done it will look something like this…

Now I want to mix it into the soil to amend the clay. Now listen, its 95 degrees while I'm doing this and climbing to 100 degrees. So while double digging this into the soil with a shovel is a great thought… I think I'll just pull back out the tiller for now…

Okay, the tilling is done..

At this point I want to kill off the grass in the middle of the keyhole and the area that borders the growing area to prevent any persistent grass from trying to creep into the growing areas.

As a side note, we will be adding a Comfrey board along with some perennial vegetables. This boarder will prevent grass from getting into the growing area while at the same time providing food and medicine.

Be sure you are subscribed to our tips newsletter so I can send you updated pictures on the progress of this new growing area.

Simply go to www.SurvivalistVictoryGarden.com/43FREE

Okay, let's continue. The first thing to do to kill off the grass is to lay out some cardboard. Make sure the cardboard has no tape on it.

Spread out the cardboard over the area you want to cover…

Make especially sure that you overlap the cardboard and that you leave no space of visible grass. Grass and weeds are opportunist. If you leave even a needle size hole for grass to come through, it will come through.

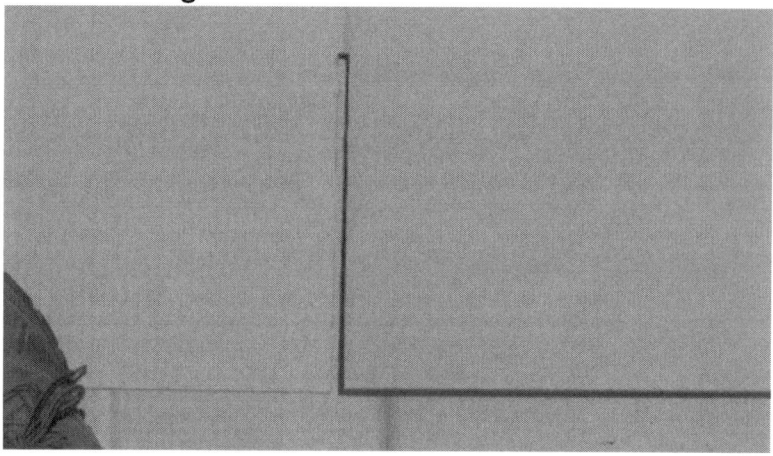

Once you have your first row of cardboard down, you want to put a pile of mulch or compost on top of the cardboard. In this case we are using mulch. We used compost on other areas.

Keep loading the mulch or compost on and use a rake to spread it out as shown below. Also shown in the picture below is the cardboard at the top on the opposite side of that growing area.

Spread your mulch or compost to complete cover the cardboard as shown in in the picture below where the keyhole area is almost completed.

The area in the center of the keyhole isn't lost space. It's actually multifunction space.

You can use this area to allow your vining crops the room to do their thing without the risk of smothering out other crops.

You can put raise beds on top of the mulched/composted area.

You can put a bird bath there to attract birds to eat bugs.

You can put a bench there to see on and admire your produce or sit there and grab snacks from your product and enjoy the outdoors.

Not every inch of grown needs to be a growing area because when you know how to grow right, you can grow big even in small spaces.

Right now, we are focusing on the lateral growing area. Shortly we will get to setting up the vertical growing area in this space.

Let's continue…

Now the top area is cover with mulch and has been distributed evenly across the cardboard.

And now we will pour out the landscape growers mix into the growing areas.

Once pour, we want to use a rake and spread it evening across the row.

I like to complete one growing area at a time so let's continue with this spot. What follows will be repeated for the other two growing rows that will complete the keyhole.

Now we want to pour on the Azomite.

And using your hands, a rake, shovel or garden weasel you want to mix the Azomite into the top 5 inches of your growing area.

Okay, so it's time to put on the Sea Mineral Solids and the Biochar. But first I like to mix them both together in a bucket. Seen below are 4 lbs of Biochar and ¾ pounds of Sea Mineral Solids.

Mix them together really good. Shown below is not really good…

Now this is really good. The Sea Mineral Solids practically disappear in the Biochar and that's the kind of mixture you're looking for.

No spread it evenly anywhere from ½ inch to 1 inch think on top of your growing area.

Mix it in real good so that it basically disappears into the top 5 inches of your growing area. You can then top of the area with some top soil. Because of how light the Sea Mineral Solids, Biochar and Azomite are, putting some top soil (optional) on it will prevent any heavy winds from sweeping away your good stuff.

Sure, all those awesome ingredients are mixed into the soil, but some of it will still be on top and hey, I want every grain of what I apply to be there.

So once you cover your growing area with top soil (optional) it will look something like this.

Now I'm going to do the right side of the keyhole. This time I'll show you another way to get your soil ready as well as add a trellis for those delicious vining and climbing crops.

So, if you want to suppress weeds within the growing area, instead of using a weed block, lay down some cardboard right where you plan on planting.

After you lay down the cardboard be sure to soak it and I mean soak all of the cardboard where it's drowning in water.

Once your cardboard is soaked, immediately lay down your compost or whatever growing mix you will be using.

Spread the growing mix evenly across the row on top of the cardboard.

Now lets' create a trellis. To do that, all you need are CMC Steel 6 foot "T" Post and some trellis netting. I HIGHLY recommend the Dalen Gardeneer Trellis Netting which is only $5 for a 5 foot tall and 15 foot wide net. You'll need a T Post Driver too. Once you drive the 6 foot T Post into the ground you will have a 5 foot higher trellis.

Position your first T Post where you want it and with your T Post Driver hammer it into the ground.

When it's don't you will have a 5 foot high post.

Go across to where you want the other end of your trellis. This is our 4th trellis. This one is around 10 feet wide. We have two trellises that are 25 feet wide one and another one that is 15 feet wide.

So based on how wide you want you trellis, make sure you get the right size trellis netting.

No sleep the trellis netting over one side of the T Post.

Next, get some Weather Resistant Zip Ties

And using 5 zip ties per post, tie down the first side.

After you complete the first side, walk over to the other T Post with the netting and slip the netting through the hoops over the post.

Now to complete your trellis, you want to pull the netting tie and until you see it is firm and it feels tight. Then using zip ties to lock in the tight position.

Now, using some scissors or a box cutter cut off the excess netting and put it away to use for a smaller trellis you may want to create.

And there you have it. A year round, weather resistant trellis ready to support pounds and pounds of delicious victory garden produce.

Okay, Now that your victory garden growing area is almost ready, let's get the seeds started.

Ready?

Let's go start some seeds…

# 3. Starting Your Seeds Step-By-Step

Okay, with your Survivalist Victory Garden growing area ready for your seeds, let's go through the process of starting your seeds.

Here's what you'll need to get started.

- You'll want a sheet to record the name of your seeds, your starting date and the date you transplant them.
- You also want some popsicle sticks to record the name of the seeds so you can label them in your seed starter.
- A fingernail filer for larger seeds.
- And of course all the seeds you will be planting.

While we have tons of stuff we are looking to plant for fall 2013. This early bunch here consists of Perpetual Spinach Chard, Welsh Onions, Comfrey and French Sorrel.

All four of these are perennials that will be used in a boarder around the growing area you saw be created in the previous chapter.

This batch also includes Beefsteak Tomato, California Wonder Peppers, Golden Acre Cabbage, Lincoln Pea, Black "Turtle" Beans and Chickpeas.

We are actually starting 2 rows each of the Black Beans and Chickpeas. More on that in a moment.
Right now, we need to prepare our soil for starting our seeds in.

I'm going to use a mixer of potting soil, biochar and sea mineral solids. This makes for outstanding soil and a very healthy environment for your seeds to start in.

We use 16 cups of potting soil to 1 cup of biochar and 2 teaspoons of sea mineral solids.

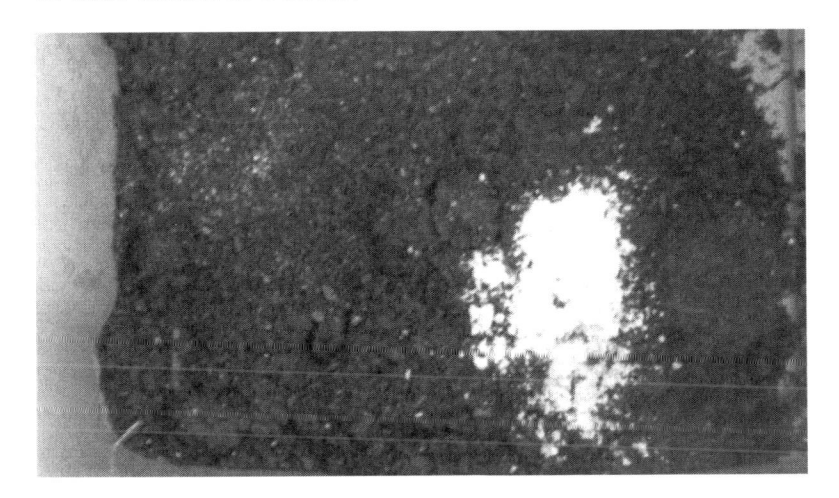

With your hands, get in there and mix it up real good.

Get the mix to where everything is blended and you can no longer distinctly see the black biochar or the sea minerals.

Okay, with our soil all see we want to prepare our growing tray. We use the Hydrofarm CK64050 Germination Station with Heat Mat. You want to pour in 46 ozs of warm clean filtered water into the tray.

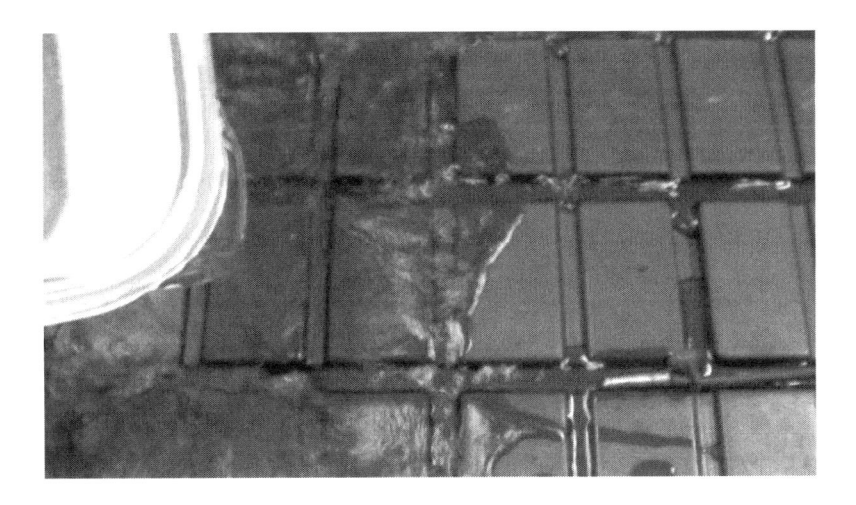

Then place the seedling inserts tray so that the water is now inside of each of the seedling cells waiting for our soil.

No take your soil mixture and start filling in all of your seedling cells.

Make sure you pat the soil down but do not stuff it in. You want the soil to be firm but loose so that the seedling can push through.

The Hydrofarm CK64050 Germination Station with Heat Mat has 72 seedling cells. So now that they are all filled with our soil, we want to start the first seed.

We want to have our pen, a popsicle stick, a sheet to record the data and of course, our seeds. I'm going to start with Perpetual Spinach Chard which is a great perennial that will keep feeding your year after year after year.

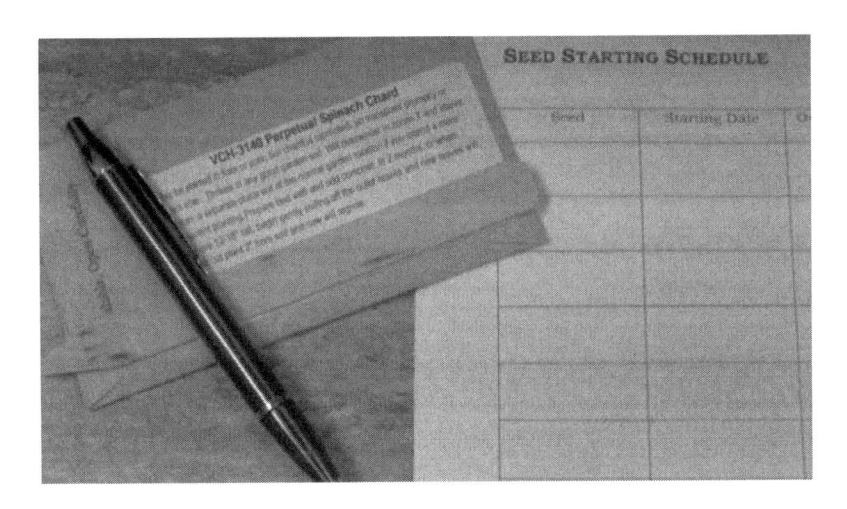

As you can see, I have labeled the popsicle stick and on my recorded I write the name of the seed and the date that we are starting these seeds.

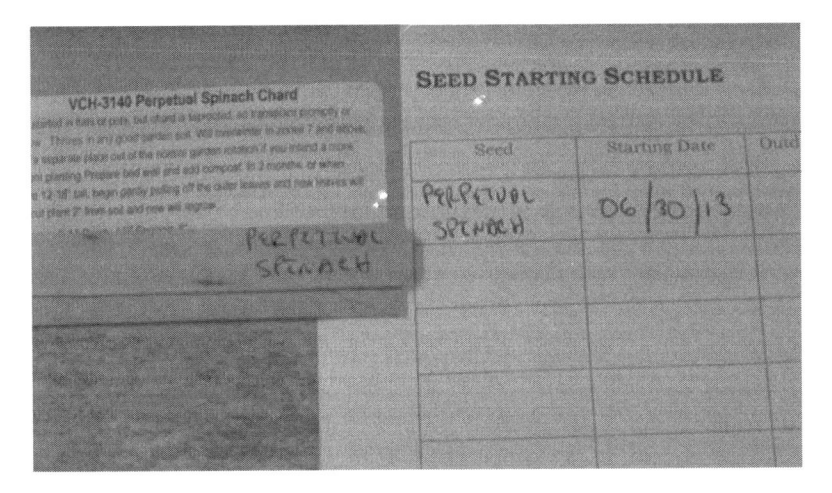

Now let's prepare the cells for the seeds. This tray has 12 rows across and 6 rows deep. So for each seed I like to plant 12 seeds with two seeds in each row of 6. To make a little space to drop your seeds in, use something like a coffee stirrer like the one in the picture below and just open up a little bit of space so that the seeds drop.

Here are some Perpetual Spinach Chard seeds

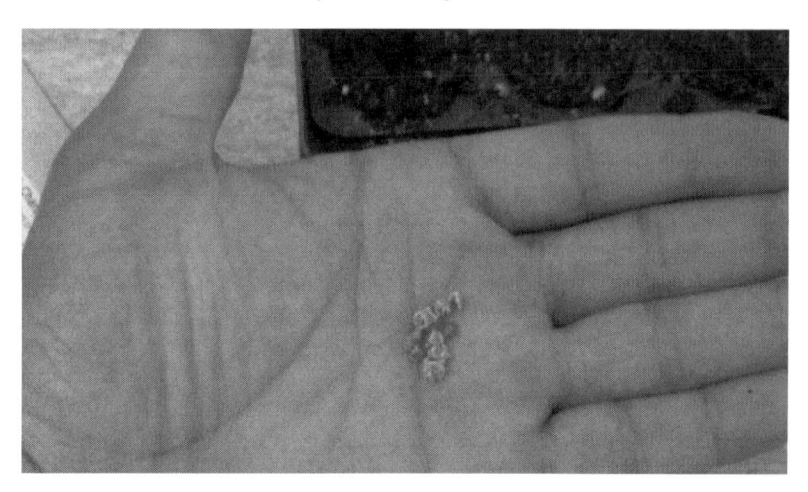

Now let's drop two inside the first cell.

Once they are in, just cover them up softly. Don't push hard on the top as you don't want any compaction that would create too much resistance to the seeds germinating and sprouting up.

Once you complete each seedling cell in that room, then take the popsicle stick and slide under that front of the row so you know what's germinating there.

Complete this process for all of your seeds, for each cell in each row. If you don't have one of these seed starting and germination sets, then I'll show you another effective way to start your seeds in just a few minutes.

For now, when you have larger seeds like peas and beans, you can use a fingernail file on them.

What you want to do is create some scars on the seeds by scraping the seeds against the fingernail file.

When you do that, you will see that part of the outer layer of the seed has been removed. This will allow the moisture to get into the seeds faster which accelerates the germination of the seeds.

Once all your seeds are completed, double check to make sure all of them are covered with soil and that each row is properly labeled for seed identification purposes.

Once you confirm that, you can place the dome over the germination tray and let God's principle of sowing and reaping go to work for you.

Now, another way to start your seeds is to use a 3 inch pot.

Make sure the pot has holes in the bottom.

Put your soil into the pot.

Get your seeds.

Put your seeds into the pot and cover them with soil.

Next, get a plastic zip-lock bag and put it over the 3 inch pot. Be sure to close the zip-lock as much as you can so the plastic bag is gripping the pot.

Now, get a small bowl of warm clean purified water.

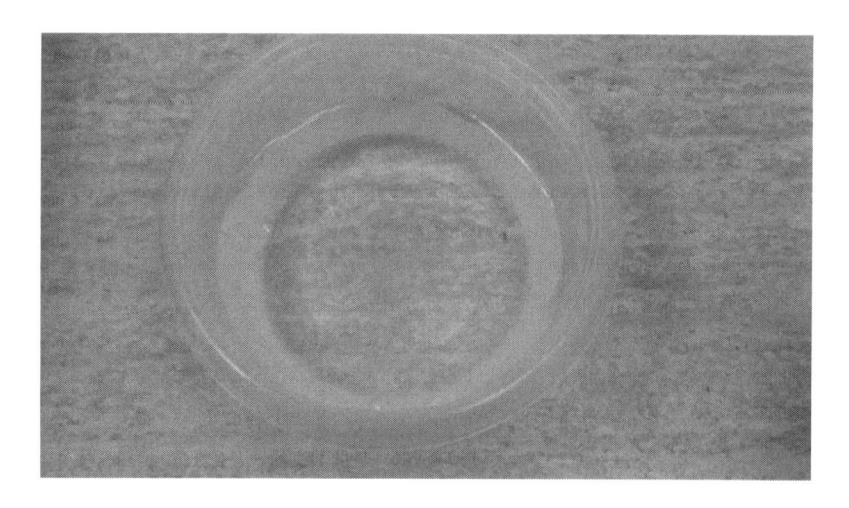

Next, simply place the 3 inch pot, with the plastic cover into the bowl of water.

This method will prevent you from over watering. Also, once the seeds germinate and develop roots the roots will be bottom fed the water.

All you want to do is make sure you keep ¼ in to ½ inch of warm clean and purified water in the bottom tray. Allow the water to dry out before refilling it.

Be sure you are subscribed to our tips newsletter so I can send you updated pictures on the progress of these seeds as well as other victory garden updates and pictures.

Simply go to www.SurvivalistVictoryGarden.com/43FREE

# 4. Crops to Grow in Your Victory Garden

A Victory Garden is a great way to utilize your idle land and to spend your free time on. Here, you can grow a wide array of vegetables and fruit trees that are suitable for your space, soil type, and climate. From grains and carbohydrates-rich crops to protein-rich crops – everything is dependent on what you want to grow and what you need to eat. Here are some of the best crops to grow in a Victory Garden and definitely some of the staple foods we need.

*Barley*

This type of grain is a good crop option to grow in a Victory Garden. It is very low maintenance and can actually thrive in just about anywhere. Additionally, this grain is adaptive to most soil types and most climates making it a great option wherever you are in the world. This can cover for your calorie needs for each day and can be used in many other ways as well. However, barley requires a lot of space to grow and needs special harvesting and processing. If you have more room in your backyard for barley to grow, this is definitely a great crop to consider.

*Beans*

Another great option to consider growing in your Victory Garden is beans. Beans can seriously grow anywhere and there are varieties you can choose to grow in different seasons. Soybean is one popular option that is very easy to produce. It is a protein-rich vegetable that can be used in many different dishes, and can be eaten in multiple ways. Moreover, soybeans actually have the capacity to make the soil where it is grown more fertile and nutritious. A cup of soybeans also contains 380 calories, making it a great alternative for your source of energy each day.

Field beans are another beans options you may want to grow in your Victory Garden. Most types of field beans are very adaptive to whatever environment they are grown. Also, field beans can store really well and will last for months if stored properly. It also contains high amounts of calories (610-660 calories per cup) and is a good source of protein.

*Beets*

Beets are also a good crop to grow in a Victory Garden. It is packed with so much nutrients and vitamins and store really well. The beet tops or greens can be cooked prepared in a variety of dishes and contain high amounts of vitamins and minerals. The beet roots, on the other hand. can be used in a handful of dishes and contain high amounts of important minerals.

*Berries (I know, I know… it's fruit. But still… ☺ )*

Berries grow at certain seasons of the year only but they are packed with antioxidants, making them a valuable addition to your garden. They also contain high amounts of vitamin C that helps fight free radicals to keep your body healthy and free from disease. From blueberries to strawberries and raspberries – they make a great addition to any garden. However, berries may be more delicate to grow than the other crops mentioned. They grow in certain climates and at certain seasons only. They also don't store really well and must be consumed immediately.

*Carrots*

For a great source of vitamins and minerals, carrots are highly suggested by gardeners and experts. Carrots contain high amounts of various vitamins and minerals making it one of the most nutritious vegetables there is. It is an excellent source of beta carotene that is helpful in fighting free radicals and in keeping the eyes healthy. Carrots are also very easy to grow and can store really well.

*Garlic*

Garlic is definitely one of the most used herbs in the world. It is used in many different dishes to add flavor and aroma. There are even some cultures that use garlic as a staple food ingredient. This is another great crop option because garlic is used in almost all dishes, anyway. This is so you won't have to constantly drive to the market just to get your supply of garlic.

Furthermore, garlic is known to contain high amounts of nutrients to help fight various diseases. It contains high amounts of antioxidants that fight free radicals that can cause cancer. It also has vitamins and minerals to keep the body healthy and strong. Garlic is one of the many herbs that can grow in a variety of climates and also stores really well lasting a few months.

*Potatoes*

Potatoes are certainly one of the first root crops that you should consider growing in your Victory Garden. Potatoes are known to contain high amounts of carbohydrates which can definitely provide for your daily needs. Moreover, potatoes are fairly easy to cultivate and grow and can actually grow in a variety of climates, too.

Aside from that, potatoes are one of the most versatile root crops you can plant that can be turned into a variety of dishes. From a simple mashed potato to more complex recipes such as pies and stews – potatoes are definitely a staple in every home. Since you will mostly be needing potatoes every day, growing them in your garden is truly a great way to use your land.

*Peas*

Peas, just like soybeans, are great to plant in your garden because they have the ability to make the soil where they are grown more fertile and nutritious. This is because peas and soybeans are both nitrogen-fixing legumes, which is an important process for the soil to keep it healthy and nutritious. Furthermore, peas are packed with lots of vitamins and minerals that make it a valuable addition to your garden. They are also very easy to grow.

These fruits and vegetables should definitely be considered when thinking of the crops to grow in your Victory Garden. The mix already provides you with all the nutrients, vitamins, and minerals you will need to survive every day. With all these in your garden, you will never have to worry about going to the market to buy your food supply. By having these in your garden, you already have your daily requirements for carbohydrates, proteins, vitamins, and minerals amply covered.

*Questions.*

Why is garlic a good crop to plant in your garden?
- Because it is used in almost all dishes and has great nutritional benefits

What fruits are great to plant in a Victory Garden?
- Berries

Which vegetables are great to grow that can make the soil more fertile?
- Soybeans and Peas

What is a great root crop to plant that contains high amounts of calories?
- Potatoes

What is a great source of complex carbohydrates to plant in a Victory Garden?
- Barley

# 5. 7 Persistent Produce (Perennial Vegetables That Keep On Giving)

Perennial plants are plants that live for two years or more. They usually bloom during summer and die back during autumn and winter. However, their root systems remain alive during those cold months. This allows them to shoot back up when spring comes.

Most perennial crops do not flower during their first season. That's because the plant concentrates on growing its roots so it can make it through the cold. This can easily discourage those who are new to growing perennial plants. However, some nurseries offer established perennials. Once transplanted, these established plants will flower during their first season.

Perennial plants are great for victory gardens because they serve as a food source that can last for decades. Some of the best perennial crops to grow are:

- Sorrel

Sorrel is a garden herb with a lemony or sour berry taste. It is a tough herb that can survive through USDA Zone Three. The plant goes by many names including Spinach Dock, French Sorrel and the Narrow-leaved Dock.

When growing Sorrel, it's best to plant it early in the spring. It needs a lot of sunlight and water, and must be divided every few years to thrive. Outdoors, it's best to plant it 1/2in deep into the ground and at least 3in apart. Indoors, it's best to grow it in 6in – 8in pots.

Sorrel can be used in several recipes. It's great in salads and springtime soups. It can also be used for fish and sauces. Some even use the leaves to make Sorrel tea. The thinnings of this plant taste fresh and tart, but once it flowers, the leaves can taste bitter.

- Egyptian Walking Onions

Egyptian Walking Onions are interesting plants to have in any garden. They grow bulblets at the tip of their stalks instead of flowers, as normal alliums do. As the bulblets grow, they weigh down the plant until it reaches the ground. From there, roots will grow and the process continues; hence the term "walking onions".

Egyptian Onions are quite hardy as they can live through USDA Zone 5. To start growing the plant, the bulblets must be planted at least 2 inches deep in well-drained soil. It is best to plant them in autumn to get them ready for spring. However, they can be planted any time of the year, even during winter as long as the ground isn't too wet or frozen. The plants must be spaced at least 6in – 10in, but they can be grown in pots as well.

The entire plant is edible and is a milder and sweeter substitute for regular onions. The unusual nature of the Egyptian Onion is also a great conversation piece.

- Garlic

Garlic gives a tasty pungent kick to any dish, but it is also excellent for growing because of its medicinal properties. The plant is a great perennial herb for beginners because it can live through USDA Zone 9.

Garlic is usually planted in mid-autumn or at least 6 weeks before the ground is expected to freeze. The bulbs must be separated into individual cloves which are planted about 3in – 4in into the ground. Garlic plants have been found to repel small animals like rabbits or moles; hence, they can be used as borders.

- Collard Greens (And Tree Collards)

Collard Greens are green leafy vegetables that belong in the same group as broccoli and cabbage. It is cultivated for its thick and slightly bitter leaves. Age does not affect the flavor of its leaves, but they are best picked before they reach their maximum size. They are also best cultivated in the cold months for maximum flavor and nutrition.

Collard Greens can be planted in spring until mid-autumn. They are heavy feeders and require a lot of nutrients. They do well when growing with high-nitrogen blend fertilizer. Regular fertilizer may also be used but they have to be fed two to three times during the summer. It is also best to space the seeds at least 2 feet apart so they won't compete for nutrients. However, they only need to be planted just a quarter of an inch under the surface.

Collard Greens have a high Vitamin A, C and K content. They also have considerable amounts of calcium, manganese and folic acid. Larger leaves are cooked and paired with smoked and salted meats. The smaller leaves can be eaten raw and added to salads.

- Asparagus

Asparagus has a delicate flavor making it great for dishes. However, its diuretic property also allows it to be used for medicinal purposes. The use of Asparagus has been traced to date back to 3,000 BC, during the time of the ancient Egyptians.

The plant grows best under full sunlight and in soil that quickly warms up. Its roots can easily rot in standing water so make sure the soil drains well. Asparagus takes time to grow, so it's best to buy established crowns for a 1 year head start. These must be planted at least 6in deep and 2ft apart.

Asparagus plants are monoecious which means individual plants are either male or female. Male plants are more productive and are best if the goal is to get a high yield. Examples of primarlly male Asparagus plants are the Jersey Giant and the Jersey Knight.

- Rhubarb

Rhubarb is an early spring herb cultivated for its tarty yet sweet flavored stalks. It is often cooked with sugar to create jams, jellies, pies and other desserts.

Rhubarb is usually grown from crowns instead of seeds. They grow best under the sun and in well-drained soil. Planting holes must be three feet wide and the crowns should be planted at least 3in deep. The plant can grow in USDA Zone 8, depending on the cultivar.

- Kale

Kale belongs to a group of green or purple-leafed vegetables such as cauliflower and Brussels sprouts. It can be grown in any season but it tastes best during the cold months, particularly when it's been touched by a bit of frost.

Like other perennials, Kale loves sunlight and well-drained soil. The plant should be spaced around 12in – 15in apart and must be planted at least half an inch deep into the soil.

Kale greens are perfect additions to salads, especially when paired with strong flavors such as almonds, pepper and Asian-style dressings. Kale handles cold temperatures well and can be stored up to a week in the fridge.

A lot of time and money is needed to successfully grow perennial crops. However, these crops will yield excellent returns in the long run. Still, novice gardeners should consult experts before starting their own perennial gardens.

Here are a few questions to see how much you've learned:

1. How are Egyptian Walking Onions different from normal alliums?

2. Why is garlic a good border?

3. What fertilizer is best for Collard Greens?

4. Asparagus is monoecious. How does this affect asparagus selection?

5. When is the best time to cultivate kale?

Here are the answers:

1. Egyptian Walking Onions grow bulblets at the tip of their stalks. Normal alliums grow flowers.

2. Garlic is known to repel small animals such as rabbits and moles, making them a good border.

3. Collard Greens are heavy feeders; this means they need nitrogen-rich fertilizers.

4. Monoecious means individual plants are either male or female. Male plants give higher yields; hence, they should be selected if that is the gardener's goal.

5. Kale is best cultivated when it's been touched by some frost.

# 6. How To Grow Crazy Giant Vegetables Naturally (Become King Of The Crops)

People associate size with wellness and quality; the same is true with vegetables. When people see giant vegetables, what they often think is the high quality and huge amount of work associated with it.

The comments that you'll hear will range from "it must have been nurtured well to grow up that big!" to "wow, she really has a green thumb." And yet, people don't know that there are actually ways to grow giant vegetables even if you're a novice, so long as you know some things, the right things. Learn more about growing giant vegetables and read on!

What Is Sea Energy Agriculture?

Sea energy agriculture is a means of getting the nutrients of seawater into the plants and animals you eat through putting them as a fertilizer.
If you are wondering how this idea came up, read on!

Sea water has a lot of mineral content that can help the plants grow in the best way possible. When seawater is used as plant food instead of being just used as a fertilizer, the plant you eat is able to fully absorb the nutrients and trace elements. Sea water is jam-packed with important minerals composed of 92 elements in the water and 84 elements in the unrefined salt.

This is a technique used by some organic farmers to ensure that their plants remain healthy. This can be beneficial for you and for the animals too. When you eat this nutrient-filled vegetable, the minerals are transferred to you. The same goes with animals that you eat.

How to Use Sea Solids

Some find the inconvenience of selling and buying sea nutrients in its liquid state, hence the introduction of sea solids.

Sea solid are dried seawater minerals. They are used by applying the same at 500 - 3000 lbs/acre. Under ordinary circumstances, one application would already last for 5 years. However, when rain water seriously washes off the sea solids, reapplication may or may not be necessary depending on the damage.

Plants provided with sea solids are said to be bigger than those which are fertilized the conventional way. Aside from being bigger in kind, the plants are more nutritious and faster to grow.

Brewing & Using Worm & Compost Tea

The initial reaction that some of you would get upon hearing the term worm and compost tea would probably be shock. After all, who would want to eat or drink something that came from worm and compost? Albeit not really appetizing, worm and compost tea can really help your plants grow healthily.

Most farmers love this technique since this type of fertilizer does not add bulk to the soil. As such, the soil remains in healthy volume while getting the nutrients it needs to bear amazing fruits.

Brewing your own worm and compost tea is possible, even if you're still a novice. All you need to have is a manual that explains all and a worm bin filled with worms.

Here are two different ways we make our compost tea.

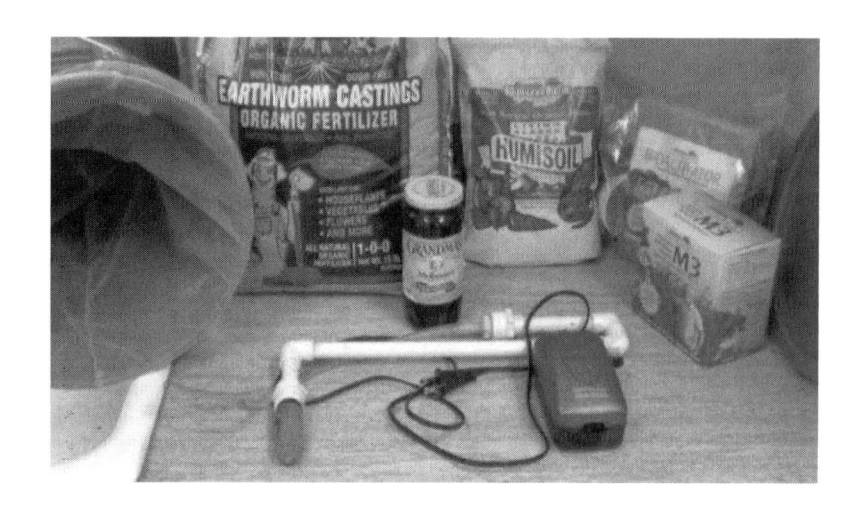

We use earthworm castings with Molasses. Make sure you are using <u>Unsulphured</u> Molasses. Also, if you want to give your worm tea or compost tea the ultimate acceleration and growth of the microbes, then add 1 teaspoon of Sea Mineral Solids per gallon of water in your tea brew.

We also use the Bountea products as shown in the picture above.

What Is ProtoGrow?

Of course, there are people who still struggle to grow giant vegetables to no avail. If you're one of those unlucky hands who is not gifted with a green thumb, don't be so hopeless, ProtoGrow is here for you!

ProtoGrow is a natural plant formula made from kelp extract and fish. With the help of this product, you're sure to make even hard-growing plants grow healthily. Moreover, there is also a claim that plants grown from this special plant formula are more delicious than those not grown with ProtoGrow. As if you need more reason, ProtoGrow is an all natural product that does not damage the soil or your health. It is completely safe for your plant. Click here to give ProtoGrow a test drive. We LOVE IT!

How to Do Foliar Feeding

Before you understand how foliar feeding works, you need to first know what foliar feeding is. Foliar feeding is the process of feeding the plant through applying a liquid fertilizer to its leaves.

Plants are totally capable of absorbing nutrients directly from its leaves. It takes place in the leaf's stomata and in the epidermis. Additionally, plant/tree barks are likewise capable of absorbing nutrients.

One of the most common versions of foliar feeding is by the use of sea-based nutrients, i.e. kelp. The reason for this is that sea-based mixes are packed with more nutrients than an ordinary organic fertilizer. Most of these sea mixes are good for the cellular formation of the leaves, and of the plant in general.

Foliar feeding works by applying the liquid fertilizer to the plant's leaves instead of the usual way of getting the fertilizer to the soil where the plant is planted.

Okay so let me walk you through how we do our foliar feeding.

While there are many different liquid fertilizers or dissolved fertilizers you can use for foliar feeding, for the purposes of this walk-thru, I show you one of the feeding combinations we use.

The process is the same, the only thing that would be different is what you are using as food in your foliar spray.

Also, please note that the directions below are for very small applications. You will want to use a much larger sprayer for larger food plots.

For example, to foliar feed all of our growing produce and over 50 fruit, nut and berries trees all we need to do is fill up a 2 gallon sprayer and a 3 gallon sprayer mix the proper amounts of food diluted in the water.

And one more thing before the quick walk-thru. We also use this same foliar mixture as an inline fertilizer in our drip irrigation system.

Okay, so let's begin.

To start we do is pull out some ProtoGrow and Sea Mineral Solids along with the sprayers. In this case a 32oz spray bottle.

You want to fill your bottle up with clean filter water.

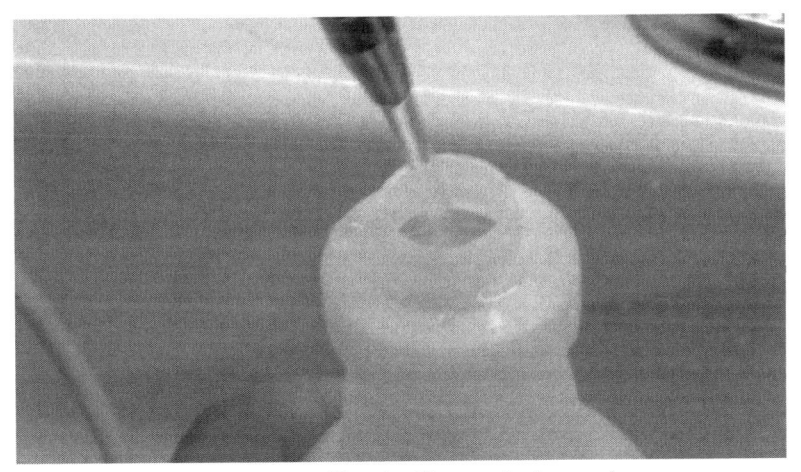

Next we pour some ProtoGrow into a 1oz cup

And then pour the ProtoGrow into the water

Next, we want 1/2 teaspoon of the Sea Mineral Solids

And we put that into the water with the ProtoGrow

Put the top back on and make sure it's tight and secure

Then shake the bottle really good for a few seconds.

Let the water sit for about 5 minutes so that the Sea Mineral Solids can dissolve into the water. After that, give it another quick shake and then go spray on top and bottom of your leaves as well as the stems and trunk like I'm doing with this baby Moringa Tree.

Plants are able to soak of the nutrients from every part, not just the roots.

In fact, here's some interesting data from a foliar applied fertilizer research trial done by The University of Michigan.

<u>Foliar Fertilization is the most efficient way to increase yield and plant health.</u> Tests have shown that **foliar feeding can increases yields from 12% to 25% when compared to conventional fertilization**.

*Tests, conducted in different locations, under different environmental conditions, have reflected the following;*

- When fertilizers are foliar applied, **more that 90% of the fertilizer is utilized by the plant.** When a similar amount is applied to the soil, only 10 percent of it is utilized.
- In the sandy loam, **foliar applied fertilizers are up to 20 times more effective** when compared to soil applied fertilizers.

*Foliar feeding is an effective method for correcting soil deficiencies and overcoming the soils inability to transfer nutrients to the plant under low moisture conditions.*

*University of Michigan - Drs. Witter and Turkey as quoted in Readers Digest magazine*

> *"... leaves lap up food like blotting paper and it spreads in a few hours from tip to root. In many cases, **as much as 95 percent of the food sprayed on the leaves is used immediately by the plant**, where under some conditions, the roots take up no more than 10 percent of the same amount placed in the soil."*

Comprehension Questions

- What makes sea agriculture a hit technique?

Sea agriculture is a big hit simply because it nurtures your plants way better than other fertilizers. Aside from helping you grow larger vegetables, sea agriculture also helps you produce tougher and healthier ones. This is because sea water contains more elements that those found in solid compost, and these nutrients are passed on to the plants you and your animals eat.

- What are the advantages of using sea solid over the usual fertilizer?

Sea solids are more preferable for both the seller and the buyer. For one, the seller would be very proud to sell high quality vegetables which he can sell at a higher price. This product can also be bought online and shipped, since it is in dry and solid form, unlike liquid fertilizers.

- What is the secret behind growing large vegetables?

The secret to growing large vegetables lies in the nutrients your plants absorb. Remember this: the minerals they are getting will show in their size. So if you want to harvest really big vegetables, try to use sea solids or natural plant formula such as ProtoGrow. Finding the right seeds can also help a lot.

- Does foliar feeding really work?

Yes, foliar feeding really works. If you look at a plant's structure, you will learn that there are also parts which can absorb nutrients such as barks and leaves because these parts have an opening which can absorb the minerals put into it.

- Is ProtoGrow safe for you and your plants?

ProtoGrow is 100% all-natural, hence it is generally safe for you and your

# 7. Unlocking Your Super Soil

## What You Should Know about Sea Mineral Solids as Fertilizer

If you are into organic farming or gardening, you should consider using **sea mineral solids** or sea salt as fertilizer.

The use of sea minerals as fertilizers started when Dr. Manday Murray became interested in the plants and animals that live in the sea. He wondered why marine life does not suffer from diseases, unlike animals and plants on land that have numerous types of diseases.

He came up with the theory that it is all because of the minerals that are present in the sea. He conducted studies and experiments that proved that all of the minerals found on earth are concentrated in the ocean water, which makes sea water the perfect fertilizer.

### *What are sea mineral solids?*

Sea mineral solids are a kind of organic fertilizer made up of sea minerals that are found to be beneficial to plants. Today, farmers and gardeners use the traditional NKP fertilizer that is only made up of three minerals, namely—nitrogen, potassium, and phosphorus.

On the other hand, sea mineral solids contain more than 92 minerals – of which, some of them are not yet identified by science. You can find the same minerals in all seawater all over the world. This means that your sea mineral fertilizer will contain the same kinds and proportions of minerals no matter which part of the world you got them from.

Initially, the fertilizer comes in liquid form. However, Dr. Murray realized that it is more difficult and expensive to transport liquid fertilizer than solid fertilize. This makes it less accessible to people who live far from the coast. Dr. Murray experimented with sea mineral solids or sea salts. He diluted them with water and used the solution as fertilizer. The result was the same as that of liquid sea mineral fertilizer.

## *Where are they from?*

Sea mineral solids come from the sea. His first experiments included seawater collected by the US Navy from the different parts of the Atlantic Ocean. He also sampled seawater from other oceans and seas. Based on these experiments, he concluded that you can use seawater from different parts of the world and get the same positive results.

The minerals come from the top layer of the sea bottom deposited by powerful rivers from different parts of the world. This is the reason why the seawater contains all kinds of minerals.

## *What are the benefits to survival gardening?*

The use of sea mineral solids as fertilizer for your survival garden offers a lot of benefits to its production and sustainability. Survival gardening is focused mainly on growing plants that can sustain a family for many years after major disastrous events such as the apocalypse or a nuclear warfare. Below is a list of benefits that you can get from using sea mineral solids in your survival garden.

- Staple crops like wheat, rice, corn, oats, and soybeans respond positively to sea mineral fertilizer according to studies. These staple crops should be a part of your food supply because they have a long shelf life and can be stored for several years. The food that you can make using these crops also keeps you from going hungry for a longer time than other kinds of food. Just make sure that you know how to properly store these food staples to make them last for as long as possible.

- When these plants are fertilized with sea mineral solids and are then eaten by animals, they will also get the minerals that the plants obtained from the organic fertilizer. And when these animals are consumed by humans, people will likewise get the same kinds of minerals. This is also true when humans eat the plants directly. These minerals are beneficial to your health and can fight certain diseases. It is important not to be sick in a post-apocalypse period when there is still chaos and doctors and medicines may not be available.

- Moreover, animals that eat plants fertilized with sea minerals mature faster and are healthier. Plants also tend to yield more when fertilized with sea minerals. This means more food supplies for your family that can help you survive for a long time.

- As long as there are still oceans in this world, you can still get these sea mineral solids and use them as fertilizers. Apocalypse or not, you can be sure that your sea mineral fertilizer will still be available because the oceans do not get easily destroyed even by nuclear war or apocalypse.

- Sea mineral fertilizer is organic. This means that it will leave very little carbon footprint which is not harmful to the environment. This also promotes soil sustainability, which means that the soil will still be in optimum condition even after many years of using the organic fertilizer. When you use artificial fertilizer, traces of chemicals will remain in the soil that will make it unsuitable for gardening or farming in the future. This can be prevented if you use sea mineral solids.

### *How do you use sea mineral solids?*

Sea mineral solids are diluted in water. It is important to dilute the sea mineral solids to prevent salt concentration on plants. You can use about 1000 to 2200 pounds of sea salt per acre. Follow the instructions on the product for the ratio of sea salt to water.

It is best to apply the fertilizer early in the morning, although it is also okay to apply it at night. You can apply it directly in the soil or on the leaves. For foliar application, you need to dilute the sea salt in more water. Depending on the situation, you can apply the sea fertilizer every month or once a year.

It is best to apply your sea mineral fertilizer separate from the other fertilizers that you are using. This is to ensure that the substances in the fertilizers do not react against each other. Again, it is best to follow the instructions in the product label or you can ask the fertilizer shop how to properly use sea mineral solids as fertilizer to achieve positive results.

# 8. A Breakthrough To Bigger & Better Tasting Everything

**Biochar – The Old New Normal for Survival Gardening**

The lowly charcoal is on a path to prominence; this time not on the grill to cook your food but on the soil as biochar, an enviable soil amendment that will help your plants grow fuller and healthier.

Biochar is the name they coined for this charcoal product that is purposely for use as soil amendment. It is derived from biomass materials such as dried twigs and trunks of plants, agricultural wastes such as wood chips, leafy greens, grass, rice hulls, coconut shells, cornhusks, and other agricultural crop residues.

Biochar is produced the same way all other charcoals are produced using pyrolysis the process of heating biomass materials in the absence of oxygen until they are carbonized. What results is fine grain charcoal, which is then spread over the soil to regenerate it.

## *Using Charcoal is an Age Old Soil Generation Technique*

Believe it or not but even long before Columbus discovered America, man has been using charcoal to make the soil fertile enough to plant crops. There is no better proof to attest to this fact except the extremely fertile and infamous Terra Preta area in the Amazon basin where the soil has remained fertile up to today for the past 2,500 years.

An analysis of the Terra Petra soil showed the presence of charcoal which experts believed is the very reason why the soil here have remained healthy all these years despite the fact that in the outlying areas around it the soil was unfit for planting crops. It only goes to show that the natives of the Amazon basin have long known this secret to a healthy soil and have used this knowledge to their great advantage to survive the harsh challenges of life.

**The Advent of Modern Agriculture made Biochar look Primitive**

Industrialization brought profound changes to agriculture. The advent of fertilizers, pesticides, and modern farm machineries and implements have significantly changed the agricultural landscape so much so that the use of charcoal to enrich soil has been relegated to the sidelines if not totally forgotten by farmers the world over.
By modern standards, the use of charcoal as a soil amendment was considered primitive.

With the modernization, the level of efficiency of agricultural production improved dramatically while profits soared. This encouraged farmers to plant more land and at an ever increasing frequency. However, the frequent planting ultimately depleted the soil of vital nutrients needed to sustain healthy plant growth and increase crop yield rendering some land useless for planting after a while.

Unfortunately, the fertilizers and pesticides that came with modernization and regaled to improve harvest also yielded a flurry of devastating health conditions among men as the harmful chemical components they contain managed to find their way into our bodies through the food produced with use of these soil amendments.

The spread of modern agriculture also did little to stem the emission of greenhouse gasses that gravely contribute to climate change. Some fertilizers in fact compounds our problems with climate change because they release Nitrous Oxide $NO^2$ (another greenhouse gas) into the atmosphere.

*The Re-emergence of Biochar as an Invaluable Soil Amendment*

Bolstered by the growing preference for things organic among the now more health conscious consumers and aided by the urgency to contribute to the effort to slow down climate change, people have become more enthusiastic about re-creating the glory days of the Terra Petra soil in the Amazon Basin where ever they can.

From the large-scale farmers to the backyard survival gardener, the use of biochar is slowly but surely permeating into the agricultural sector and for all the good reasons.

Here are some of them:

- Biochar nourishes the soil back to health. It is able to retain soil nutrients and water more efficiently at the same time allowing the controlled presence of microorganisms to help in enriching the soil further. Many studies have proven time and again that Biochar used as soil amendment results in more robust and healthier plants.

- When applied to the soil, biochar serves as a 'carbon sink' by holding and retaining up to 50% of the Carbon Dioxide $CO^2$ (another greenhouse gas) normally released into the atmosphere by decaying biomass in the soil. And because biochar is extremely inert and stable, it is able to perpetually retain $CO2$.

- Biochar improves water quality by retaining soil nutrients and other agrochemicals in effect preventing them from leaching and polluting our ground water supply.

- Biochar production results in better and more efficient organic waste management. Instead of leaving biomass wasted to decay as compost and release more $CO2$ into the atmosphere, they are slowly carbonized and the gasses produced by the process are diverted and used as an energy source.

- Biochar reduces fertilizer requirement by 10%.

- Biochar raises the soil's pH and reduces acidity while enhancing soil microbial respiration.

*Biochar is an Invaluable Solution to Survival Gardening Too*

Another emerging lifestyle concept that is fast becoming popular is survival gardening. Simply put, it is about planting your own food in your own backyard or in whatever available space imaginable. It stems from the need to insure you have a continuous supply of food even if unforeseen events hamper the normal food distribution channels.

It goes without saying that with very limited space available to raise your vegetables and other plant food, using biochar-enriched soil is the most logical alternative. Not only will it nourish whatever soil you use, it will also keep it fertile for a long time.

*The proper use of Biochar*

For large-scale applications, a minimum of 50 Mega grams (Mg) ($10^6$ grams) of biochar per hectare is recommended. As a rule of the thumb, biochar should be no more than 30% of the soil mass. Biochar can be spread over the soil surface, mixed with mulch or compost, or mixed with water and applied as liquid slurry.

For backyard survival gardening, an easy way of incorporating biochar is to put 3 parts of biochar for every 7 parts of nutrient rich potting soil you put in a container or by mixing it with compost.

Biochar is commercially available and ready to use; but if you wish, you can produce your own charcoal. There are several online sources you can browse to help you make it happen. But never use commercial charcoal for use with a griller. They contain chemicals to aid combustion that are harmful to the plants.

# 9. The Amazing Abundant Crop Producer

## Azomite and Remineralization: The Secret for Survival Gardening

### What is Azomite?

Azomite is both the trade name and an acronym for the unique mineral chemically called *hydrated sodium calcium aluminosilicate*. More properly presented in upper case letters, AZOMITE stands for **A-Z** of **m**inerals **i**ncluding **t**race **e**lements. This mineral is an ore of complex silica lauded as a miraculous rock dust with many uses. Azomite was named by Rollin Anderson, a geological prospector whose trade essentially locates the most ideal drilling sites for mining purposes.

Anderson derived his name for the unique mineral based on its composition. The pink ore originally obtained by Anderson from Utah and subjected to thorough chemical scrutiny revealed minerals of marine origin and volcanic ash. Its mineral composition showed a wide range of trace minerals and rare earth elements. Thus, with over 70 trace minerals, Anderson's choice of A-Z (i.e., A to Z) couldn't have been more apt.

The discovery of Azomite was not at all accidental. Anderson set out for rustic Utah from the then more convenient life in San Francisco for a grand purpose. He was on a quest for a yet unknown remedy for the frail and sickly Americans. He theorized that the food feeding America and the mineral-depleted soil where most of the food were grown from were making America sick and unhealthy.

Finding Azomite was not, however, a wild goose chase. Utah was home to the gypsum mine owned by Anderson's old man. His earlier theory was grounded on the utility of gypsum to enhance the alkaline-laden farms in the locality. Moreover, Anderson targeted Utah owing to Native American accounts of the mystical healing powers of the painted rocks. Today, those painted rocks are called petroglyphs, which were engraved using sharp tools by earlier men to carve images.

Anderson's knowledge of the soil would have contributed to his theory about soil depletion. However, associating soil depletion and the need for a mineral-rich remedy for the problem was brilliant. As will be revealed in the latter sections of this article, Anderson struck a mineral-mine when he found Azomite.

## Where is it from?

Azomite was discovered in Utah and is of volcanic origin. Geologic history of the Utah area where Azomite deposits are mined showed substantial parallelism with the composition of the mineral:

- The eruption of a volcano about 30 million years ago gave the mineral its volcanic ash content. Meanwhile, volcanic ash from the eruption contains rare earth elements.

- The lava and pyroclastic material that spewed from the eruption and covered a seabed in the proximity of the volcano contributed to the marine minerals in the ore examined.

- Rivers, which branched out before to the covered seabed, were known to have high mineral content.

## What are the benefits of Azomite to survival gardening?

The term survival gardening may sound apocalyptic to some. But in the simplest sense of the phrase, it may be taken to mean having fresh food on the table on a regular basis without having to spend money and buy from a grocery or supermarket.

However, from a survivalist viewpoint, it is more of a strategy for arranging plants in a large area such that even people living near your residence will hardly notice that your family has an extensive source of food supply.

The basic idea is actually borne out of dread about the SHTF scenario. Optimists look at survival gardening as preparation for the inevitable, whereas pessimists view the practice as apprehension for the unthinkable.

However one perceives survival gardening is never an issue, but the benefits of Azomite to survival gardening can never be overlooked even by the typical gardeners or the smart agriculturists.

Anyone growing plants for survival gardening would want fruits and vegetables to be bigger and heavier as much as possible. This is one of the vaunted benefits of Azomite that have been scientifically documented. Nevertheless, the greatest benefit of Azomite whether it be to survival gardening or traditional agriculture is its efficacy in the remineralization of soil.

Remineralization is the process of revitalizing the soil by emulating natural processes through the use of rock dust that originated from alluvial deposits, glaciation, and volcanic eruptions. Remineralization restores the nutrients originally found in rich soils. Since the soil is a product of
geologic processes, addition of rock dust formed from the very same processes imitates nature's way of replenishing vital elements in soil to make it productive.

Remineralization provides slow, natural release of elements and trace minerals, rebalances the pH of the soil, increases the soil's resistance to insects and disease, and promotes the production of larger and more nutritious crops. Aside from remineralization, the other benefits that can be derived from Azomite are:

- Assists in preventing acidification of soil;
- Contains major nutrients, micro-nutrients, and essential elements needed by plants in small quantities for more robust growth;
- Cures/prevents citrus blight;
- Detoxifies the human body by pulling out positively charged pathogens;
- Helps chickens produce more eggs which have sturdier shells for lesser breakage;
- Helps plants to take in essential nutrients from the soil;
- Makes pastures and hay better-preferred by animals;
- Prevents animal feed from caking;
- Promotes the growth of chicken and pig, improves their zest for reproduction, as well as immunity from diseases;
- Protects plants and their yield from infestation by worm and other insects;
- Reduces the reliance of farmers on pesticides; and
- Regarded as a superfood

**How is Azomite used?**

Here are some ways of using Azomite

- Azomite powder is edible. It is an excellent source of the minerals calcium and magnesium.
- It is used as an additive for animal grain feed.
- It is used in promoting plant growth and is a big boost to plant nurseries when added to the soil.

- It is also used in organic farming since it helps increase the nutritional level of farm products.
- Some chefs add Azomite powder to smoothies or use them when baking bread and cooking casseroles.

With more uses and application being uncovered by science and research, Azomite tops the list of chemicals with a myriad of uses. The best part of the story is, however, the very affordable cost of procuring this useful product. Its discoverer, Rollin Anderson couldn't be prouder.

# 10. A Victory Gardens Best Friend

Since the beginning of modern times, man has sought to find ways to improve the quality and quantity of the array of flowers and produce in his garden. Countless attempts at fertilizers and gardening tricks have been tried - some more successful than others.

As odd as it may seem, seaweed fertilizer is among the most prized Master Gardener tricks. We'll take a look at a brief history of how seaweed has been used in the garden as well as characteristics and uses of this most fascinating sea product.

The use of seaweed has been part of the history of seacoast countries for centuries. In England, in the Channel Islands, there is actually a trade called vraicking, where seaweed is harvested and then dried before it is sorted for different uses including fertilizer.

In times past in Ireland, the soil was lifted in rows and then seaweed was placed down before the soil was laid back down. Not practiced so much anymore, this is how potatoes were planted and cultivated. To this day, Ireland cultivates and harvests some 35,000 tons of an estimated 500+ species of seaweed and kelp as a small part of their coastal industries.

Why seaweed is such an amazing additive to gardens, then and now, is due to the fact that the world's oceans contain every element known to mankind. Naturally sea plants will avail themselves of this, which makes them an ideal amendment for the garden.

It's the popular choice for conscientious gardeners who want an all-natural plant based product to add to their soil in junction with other natural sources of fertilizer. It doesn't have the negative "news" of big industry name brand chemical synthesized fertilizers with all the questionable by-products and pollution that come with processing and manufacturing.

It's interesting to note how seaweed fertilizer is used. It can be directly added to your soil as mulch to your garden around and between the plants, although it breaks down very rapidly.

It can be added to your compost bin too, to add great richness and friability to the overall humus. It can also be made into to a "tea" either from the liquid extracts or the powder forms available. This is then misted onto the leaves as a foliar feed.

Seaweed has had a long and productive history in gardens worldwide. You may be fortunate enough to find it near your home if you live near the sea. But for the rest of you, who may not have this convenience, visit your local nursery or garden supply and ask for kelp meal or another product based on seaweed. And while you're there, ask them to give you some tips on how to add it to your garden to give it new life.

**Organic Seaweed Fertilizer Is A Victory Gardens Best Friend**

If you want to go for a blue ribbon at the fair next summer, then you may want to learn a few new gardening tricks. Perhaps you haven't heard of using organic seaweed fertilizer before - but now we'll take a look at what this humble (if not smelly) sea vegetation can do for what you grow in your garden!

Seaweeds affect the soil by building it, adding much needed minerals as well as starches that feed the humus. After discovering what seaweed can do, you may find yourself ready to head off to the local garden shop to grab a bag or bottle of this simple, yet effective fertilizer.

While seaweed and kelps have a bulky appearance when they are fresh, much like any land vegetation, when it dries, it looks sort of sad and limp. But like the land vegetation, if added to soil, it supplies a vast array of nutrients, not the least of which are alginates, which are the starches in seaweed. Although the alginates don't actually bulk up the soil much, these do act to clump soil particles and hold moisture near the roots, which is what you want.

Like tiny sponges, these starches hold onto the microscopic water droplets. Experts tell us that plants don't like "wet feet" or to have the root system not drain well. Yet moisture must be available to the roots in miniscule amounts. Enter the seaweed - a perfect answer to this problem.

A second important benefit of these alginates is that they act to feed the microorganisms that live in the soil, which in turn break down the soil so that it may be better assimilated by the roots.

Before any plant root system can take in any nutrients, these potential nutrients must be chelated or made "user friendly" for those roots. The tiny bacteria that live near the plants roots feed on these starches, which are supplied by vegetation such as seaweeds.

For anyone desiring an all-natural way to bring nutrient to their plants, seaweed products are the best choice. As you know, the sea contains a most complete array of minerals. Because of this, seaweeds are the most complete source of plant-based minerals.

It's these plant-based minerals that are more quickly assimilated by the plant's root system and therefore the whole plant. As an addition to an organic garden, kelp meal or seaweed fertilizers can make the difference between a so-so garden and a vibrant, healthy garden.

As you might expect, much like taking vitamins and minerals to help our body's health, so it goes for your garden. It's long been known that our vast farmlands' soils have been depleted of essential elements due to over-raising of crops and exhausting the soil. Seaweed, when added to the full complement of soil amendments, can improve soil and thus increase the quality and quantity of produce.

It stands to reason that by adding seaweed fertilizer to your own organic garden, you'll begin to notice amazing changes as your garden soil as well as your plants they take in the minerals and trace elements that seaweeds provide. Why not join the few who know that adding organic seaweed fertilizer to your garden can mean the difference between average output and fabulous?

## Seaweed Fertilizer with a Liquid Fish Extract

Adding fertilizer to soil has been practiced for as long as gardeners have gardened! From our history lessons, we may remember that the American Indian taught the new settlers to add fish to the holes where they were adding corn seeds.

Since then, we've found more convenient ways to use this same practice. Only now we can find fish combined with seaweed! Why a fish emulsion? Adding fish by-products to your garden brings a quick burst of nitrogen as a foliar feed.

It also brings a fair amount of P and K, too. The fish bones supply calcium, which contributes to strong cell structure and helps balance pH in the soil. When you use the combined qualities of fish emulsion and seaweed's vast army of trace elements and plant hormones, you're bound to see some positive benefits. Professional gardeners say a seaweed/fish fertilizer combo is to a plant is like pizza is to humans!

It's most common to find the components - fish emulsion and seaweed meal or extracts - separately. They come in both dried and liquid forms. But there are some brands that come with both together so look for seaweed/fish emulsions wherever you find specialty fertilizers.

As you would expect, you can find fish emulsion and seaweed fertilizer through nursery outlets. It's also available through retail establishments online. But for the do-it-yourselfer, you can try your hand at mixing up a batch at home!

Start with a large bucket that's filled halfway with sawdust and seaweed meal. Add canned or fresh fish parts then cover in a solution of water and a healthy dose of molasses and a tablespoon of Epsom salts. You'll want to cover this as it gets ripe. Stir every few days for 1 or 2 weeks.

After the brewing time, add water to dilute, then use the liquid to water your plants or to foliar feed (1:1 on the roots and 1:5 on the leaves). Then don't waste the dregs. Apply them on your garden or in your compost pile.

There are many great websites online that give greater detail on this topic. Just type "fish emulsion and seaweed fertilizer" into your favorite search engine and you'll find several sources that will provide you with more fascinating facts about fish and seaweed garden additives.

It may seem odd to those who are unfamiliar to gardening, but to those who know how soils and plants work, using a seaweed and fish mixture just makes good sense. The all-natural source of trace elements and starches in seaweed plus the high nitrogen and calcium content in fish parts make this combo a gardener's "dynamic duo."

**Seaweed Fertilizer Works Well With Container Gardening**

Plant lovers since the beginning of time have sought ways to bring the beauty and freshness of plants and greenery into and nearer the home. But with this brings a unique set of problems such as what to feed and how to feed these container plants.

Here is where seaweed fertilizers can really shine. The characteristics of seaweed are well suited to container gardening as it contains a nice balance of nutrients that you can add to your potting soil when first planting as well as regular feedings.

Master gardeners and common folks alike who love the thought of growing thriving healthy plants with the convenience of containers on their porch or patio, must concern themselves with the special needs of plants that are grown in confined quarters. A good potting soil takes this into consideration by making sure there's a proper mix of peat, tiny stones and soil.

Adding kelp meal to the mix before your plant can aid the moisture retention of the potting mix while at the same time not allowing the soil to become heavy. In this way, your plants can enjoy the benefits of the mineral content as well as the starches of the seaweed or kelp meal.

Anyone who has done container gardening for long knows that plants planted in such a way have a different need for watering than for plants grown in the ground. Since most plant roots don't like to be wet or bone dry, the container gardener must take care to add water on a timely basis.

It makes sense to add a fertilizer to the watering liquid from time to time to replace the depleted minerals and enzymes in the potting soil. Liquid forms of seaweed fertilizers are a natural form of plant supplement unlike name brand fertilizers that are a "chemical koolaid" for plants. Be sure to follow label instructions before applying.

Another way seaweed fertilizer works with potted plants is to use a diluted solution of a special extract, which is then either sprayed on the leaves of the plants or "watered" on the soil on a regular basis.

Foliar feeding as it is called is a common trick of Master Gardeners that is just becoming more prevalent as the public learns about the amazing benefits of misting the leaves of their plants, on occasion.

The tiny pores on the upper and lower sides of leaves allow the plant to take in nutrients at the source, if you will. Seaweed fertilizers have an ideal balance of nutrients that are well suited to this type of plant feeding.

You must take care to read labels to get the dilution right because you don't want to "burn" the plants. But gardeners can notice a huge difference in leaf and flower quality within days by using this special treatment.

For those who love the convenience of container gardening and also desire an all-natural plant food, seaweed fertilizer may be just the thing that's missing from your home greenhouse arsenal.

# 11. 7 Must Have Medicinal Herbs (Natures Doctor in Your Yard)

Before the advent of drugs, supplements and modern medical technology, humans depended on medicinal herbs for their health needs. Every culture or race has their own herbal medicine traditions, and many of the modern medicines and supplements today are derived from the extracts of medicinal plants.

The benefit of growing medicinal herbs in victory gardens is quite straight forward. They help keep gardeners and their families healthy, thus cutting down medical bills and prolonging life. Some of the best medicinal plants to grow in any garden are:

- Chamomile

Chamomile is a famous herbal plant used for tea. Chamomile tea is great for inducing sleep and preventing nightmares. It also has some mild pain-relieving effects which can help with stomach upset and menstrual cramps. When incorporated in creams or used topically, it can help heal and soothe bites, burns and cuts. It also helps whiten the skin.

Chamomile is also known as a physician plant. Gardeners have successfully rescued "dying" plants simply by planting Chamomile next to them. There are numerous varieties of the plant, but German Chamomile remains to be the favorite for its blossoms.

Chamomile seeds are usually planted late in the winter, around 6 weeks before the last frost. The seeds should be sprinkled on seed pots and allowed to sprout on the surface. Once the last frost is over, they can be transplanted into the garden.

Chamomile should be planted at least 12in apart. They love sunlight and can survive without additional watering. The plant can thrive on standard fertilizer and can readily seed itself.

- Lemon Balm

Lemon Balm is an herb that belongs to the mint family. When crushed and applied topically, the herb can help treat wounds and bites and acts as a mosquito repellant. When taken as a tea, it can cure bloating, vomiting, menstrual cramps and other forms of pain.

Lemon Balm also has some psychiatric and neurologic effects. It has been used to treat conditions such as anxiety, restlessness and sleep problems. It can also help improve cognitive function and fight against the symptoms of Alzheimer's disease.

Lemon Balm is usually grown in the spring or early autumn. Although it can grow through seeds, growing through root cuttings is easier and faster. Root cuttings should be planted in moist soil, 1 – 2 feet apart. The herb grows rapidly and freely, so constant cultivation may be needed to prevent it from turning into a weed.

- Mullein

Mullein is a plant that commonly grows in the wild. It's been found growing on roadsides, fields and forest openings. It is recognizable for its tall flower spikes that reach up to 10ft. Its flowers have five symmetrical petals that come in several different colors, yellow being the most common.

Mullein hates the shade and it should be grown after the last frost of spring or in the summer. When seeding, the plant should be scattered liberally on potting soil. It takes two weeks to germinate and can be transplanted outdoors once it has two leaves. The plant should be spaced at least 1ft apart and planted a quarter of an inch deep.

During its first season, Mullein will only develop a rosette of leaves that are usually 6in to 15in long. Their flowers will only appear during the second season. Leaves of the plant can be harvested as they grow and they can be used for asthma, cough and other respiratory diseases.

- Patchouli

Patchouli is a bushy herb that belongs to the mint family. It reaches up to three feet and bears small whitish-pink flowers. The herb is grown mostly for its strong fragrance and is often used in the production of oils and perfumes.

Patchouli also has several medicinal uses. When its oil is used in aromatherapy, the herb can help reduce stress and alleviate depression. Its antibacterial properties make it excellent for use as a mouthwash, deodorant and a treatment for wounds.

Patchouli is native to tropical countries, which means it loves warm weather. However, it prefers to grow under the shade. It grows best on moist soil that drains well and has a pH level of 5.5 to 6. Patchouli can be bought as seeds but they are easier to grow when bought as seedlings. The seedlings should be planted at least 2 feet apart to allow them to grow. The plant will not survive during cold climates so it should be covered with blankets during fall or winter.

- Valerian

Valerian is a perennial plant known for its sweet scented flowers. It was used primarily in the production of perfumes in the sixteenth century. Today, it is recognized for numerous medicinal purposes.

Valerian is often used in combination with hops and lemon balm to cure insomnia. It can also alleviate psychiatric problems such as anxiety, stress and phobias. Its mild pain-relieving effects can help treat migraines, stomach aches and joint pains.

Native to marshes and streams, the Valerian grows well in moist soil. It can thrive in full sunlight or partial shade. The plant can be hard to grow from seeds so novice gardeners should consider buying established plants.

When planting Valerian, they must be spaced at least 3in apart. Their roots emit a pungent odor that can attract rats, dogs and cats. To prevent them from being dug up, it's important to plant them firmly into the soil and to weigh the ground down with a few stones.

- Comfrey

Comfrey is a perennial herb with broad leaves and bell-shaped flowers. They are native to Europe and prefer to grow in damp places such as riverbanks and ditches.

The plant can be incorporated into ointments or turned into paste and used to soothe cuts, bruises and the suppuration of boils. As a tincture or tea, it can help heal respiratory and digestive diseases. It can also be used in combination with other herbs to stop internal bleeding and to help with bone healing.

Comfrey acts similar to weeds, growing fast and without much help. It will benefit much from nitrogen-rich fertilizers and neutral to acidic soil. The plant can be grown from seeds, but it takes two years to germinate. That's why most gardeners prefer to purchase established Comfrey instead.

When planting, Comfrey should be at least 3ft apart and 3in – 6in deep. Leaves should first be harvested when the plant is at least 2ft tall, but subsequent cuts can be done at any time.

- St. John's Wort

St. John's Wort is a perennial plant indigenous to Europe. It's primarily used to treat major depressive disorders, especially among teens and children. It's also been found effective for psychiatric diseases such as ADHD and OCD.

The herb is great for novice gardeners because it can grow even in poor soil and it can easily survive through cold months. Its seedlings are best planted in late spring and can be harvested in July of the next season.

Medicinal herbs are easy to grow and are fairly inexpensive. It takes some time and effort to get things started, but a week's worth of work will easily equate to years of fruitful harvests.

**Comfrey Revisted for Prepping Your Garden** *(The What Why Where and How)*

*Again… What is Comfrey?*

There are several genus of Comfrey. This includes but is not limited to common comfrey (Symphytum officinale), rough comfrey (Symphytum asperum), and the popular hybrid Symphytum× uplandum. General appearance remains constant, regardless of genus. It is a small to medium sized perennial herb with blackish roots much like a turnips. Comfrey has broad hairy green leaves, and a mild purple, violet, cream or stripped flower.

*Why is it Beneficial for Preparation Gardening?*

Comfrey, especially the hybrid types, grows deep root systems. This allows it to extract nutrients deep within the soil. It is then transferred to the many broad leaves. In other words, it is a great way to draw nutrients from deeper unused soil, and distribute them to the top. As a result, you maximize the utility of a small plot of land. This will then better the quality and quantity of crops or plants planted.

> Tip: If you are new at this, It is better to purchase the hybrid (Symphytum× uplandicum). This is because it is the hardiest and also the most versatile. Based on most consumer reports and a cursory internet search, it is also the easiest to find.

**How to Use Comfrey**

The nutrients absorbed by the roots are transferred to the leaves. It can then be utilized as:

- Compost Catalyst: Add Comfrey in moderation in compost pits. The leaves tend to liquefy. When it does liquefy, it gets converted into nitrogen. This heats up the pit and speeds up the composting process. Tip: Mix well and don't add too much since the liquefied goo can affect the moisture level of your compost pit.

- Mulch: Sometimes referred to as side dressing or side dish. This is because when used as mulch, Comfrey should be lined around the plant or crops. This way when it does decay, it releases the nutrients not too near the stem. This maximizes nutrient absorption and minimizes heat and nitrogen damage to the stem.

- Comfrey Tea: Arguably the simplest method of extraction. All you have to do is soak a few dozen of leaves in a pail of water. Leave it there for 4 to 5 weeks. The resulting mix can then be used to water your crops in moderation.

- Concentrate: This requires a little bit more work, but can be stored for use over long periods of time. You need to devise a drum or boxlike container with small holes on the bottom. Stack leaves inside the container, and then press weights on it. The simplest way to do this would be a contraption of plywood as a stable press and hollow blocks or heavy rocks as weights. You place a catching bowl beneath the holes. Wait a few weeks and a thick viscous fluid will drop onto the bowl. Bottle and store it. Before using the concentrate, dilute it with water. The ratio must be 15:1.

- Potting Mix: Most experts have different formulas when it comes to mixing Comfrey. The most accepted mixture is

composed of:
- Leaf mold (preferably 2 years in the making)
- Dolomic limestone
- Roughly chopped Comfrey

Mix in a bit of dolomic limestone on your un-layered mixture for a better/higher PH. Alternately layer leaf mold and comfrey several times. Each layer should be three (3) to four (4) inches thick. Keep the mixture adequately moist (not wet and not dry). It is ready in two (2) to five (5) months, or when the leaves are no longer visible/recognizable.

## Medicinal Value of Comfrey

There is no conclusive study as of yet, but most physicians will not warn against comfrey topical mixes. Studies show that Comfrey contains trace amounts of allantoin, which is good for repairing damages cells and tissue. It also has anti-inflammatory properties.

A traditional name for Comfrey is "knitbone". This is a testament to its bone mending properties when topically applied to the skin. Warning: Comfrey must only be applied topically, NEVER orally and never on deep gashes. This is because it also contains a sufficient dose of Pyrrolizidine alkaloids to harm humans.

## Survival Gardening

In any survival situation you need to plan for rescue and for the long term. Comfrey gardening is a good way to plan for the latter. Below are a couple of survival scenarios where you can best utilize Comfrey.

Situation 1: Stranded

> If you are stranded and you find Comfrey; then you can utilize it in the short term for its medicinal properties. Use it as a salve for shallow wounds and to bring down inflammation. In the long

term, you can utilize it as fertilizer when growing crops. Chances are, when you find one Comfrey you will find dozens of them, so search thoroughly. Tip: Comfrey decomposes fast, so pick only what you will use, and leave the rest for later. Try to clear the surrounding areas of weeds and debris to stimulate growth of you are growing your own Comfrey.

Situation 2: Doomsday Prepping

Preparing for a disaster is a past time that is gaining momentum. Most preppers know that you need to have a renewable resource of foodstuff. This is only possible by growing crops in small, protected locations. Using Comfrey is a great way to enrich the soil for better crops and allow year round utilization. In other words, you can minimize resting time for the soil by continually adding natural fertilizer.

Using Comfrey is a natural way to enrich the soil. And when it comes to gardening, natural and organic methods are always the best. It takes a little bit more work, but the results are always worth it!

Comfrey is truly a survivalists and preppers independence from commercial fertilizers and compost.

Here are some questions to test how much you've learned:

1. Which medicinal herb can be planted next to dying plants to revive them?

2. Which medicinal herb is known for alleviating the symptoms of Alzheimer's disease?

3. When will the flowers of Mullein start to appear?

4. Why should Valerian be planted firmly into the soil and weighed down with a few stones?

5. How can you tell when Comfrey can be harvested?

Here are the answers:

1. Chamomile. Chamomile is known as a physician plant and has been known to rejuvenate nearby plants.

2. Lemon Balm. Lemon Balm has numerous neurologic effects, including the alleviation of the symptoms of Alzheimer's.

3. During the 2nd Season. On Mullein's 1st season, only a rosette of leaves will appear.

4. Valerian emits an odor that attracts animals. Weighing it down prevents it from being dug up.

5. Comfrey can be harvested once it is at least 2 feet tall.

# 12. 4 Super Seeds for Sure-Fire Survival

Superfood is a term used to describe certain food items that have great nutritional value and numerous medical benefits. A number of food items have been granted this designation including acai berries and blueberries.

If there's a food group that deserves to be called super, it's seeds. Seeds contain a whole host of vitamins, minerals and other essential nutrients. They are extremely versatile because they can be incorporated in recipes, sprinkled on breads and salads or eaten on their own. 5 half-ounce servings of super seeds a week is enough to lower high blood pressure, ease joint pains and keep cholesterol at manageable levels. Must-have super seeds are:

- **Chia Seeds**

Chia is a flowering plant that belongs in the mint family. It is native to Mexico and Guatemala. The term chia is derived from the Mayan word "chiabaan" which means strengthening. Based on its name, it's only fitting that Chia seeds have been awarded the status of super seed.

Chia seeds are tiny black seeds believed to have been a staple part of the diets of the Mayans and Aztecs. They are rich in vitamins, minerals and other nutritious components. Health benefits of Chia seeds include the following:

- Rich in Omega-3
- Improves Digestion
- Helps with Weight Loss
- Hydrates the Body
- Reduces High Blood Pressure

Chia plants are best grown by sprouting the seeds. The seeds must be moistened in water for an hour, and then covered with foil to keep in the moisture. The seeds will germinate after four days.

Chia seedlings can be transplanted once they begin to shed their hulls. It's best to keep them under sunlight and to mist them every day. Chia seeds can easily be harvested by drying the plant's flower and beating them against a container. The seeds can be stored in a dry place until they are ready for use.

- **Flax Seeds**

Flaxseeds can be found in every grocery store, right around the cereal or supplement aisle. This seed is so ingrained in people's everyday lives that few know how beneficial it actually is for their health. Nutritionists say that its health benefits can be achieved by consuming just 1-2 tablespoons of its ground form every day. Examples of these health benefits are:

1. Prevents Cancer, diabetes and heart diseases
2. Slows down the ageing process
3. Reduces inflammation
4. Balances estrogen levels and helps ease the symptoms of menopause
5. Helps relieve constipation

The primary reason that Flaxseed is so beneficial is its high Omega-3 content. In fact, 50% of the seed is made of that fatty acid. It also contains the highest concentration of Lignan (among other seeds), a compound that is known for battling cancer.

Those who want to grow their own flaxseed plants should start with the seed. The seeds are planted in germinating pots around 5 weeks before the last frost. Once they've germinated, they can be transplanted in organic-rich soil. The seedlings must be spaced at least a foot apart. They can take time to sprout and can easily be overwhelmed by weeds. It's best to keep the area weed-free to help the plant grow.

A single flax plant will not be enough to get high yields. That's why it's not recommended to grow the plant in a container. The seeds of the plant can be harvested once the pods turn yellow. Once the seeds are dried, they can be stored for up to 10 months.

- **Moringa Seeds**

Moringa is a "miracle tree" known for its numerous nutritional and medicinal properties. Every part of the tree is either edible or used for medicine, so it's a handy plant to have around.

Seeds from the Moringa plant are in high demand around the world. It contains around 40% of Ben oil that's rich in antioxidants and has nutritional properties similar to olive oil. This non-drying oil has an indefinite shelf-life; this is in contrast with other oils that turn rancid after a while. Health benefits of the Moringa seed include:

1.  Coagulation, prevention of internal bleeding and wound healing

2.  Mild anti-inflammatory effects to soothe arthritis, cramps and gout

3.  Anti-bacterial properties that protect against wound infections, sexually transmitted diseases and boils

4.  Relaxation for patients with epilepsy

5.  Flocculant used to clear dirt, germs and worms in water to make it potable

Moringa is a highly versatile plant that can make any victory garden complete. Still, growing a tree is not as easy as growing herbs and bushes. The easiest way to grow them is from cuttings. Every year, the tree stops bearing fruit. To get fresh growth, some branches need to be cut off. These branches can be planted 3 ft deep into the ground to grow new trees. Germination through this method occurs in two weeks.

Moringa trees can also be grown from seeds. They should be planted directly in the area where they are intended to grow. Three to five seeds should be planted in a 1.5cm deep hole. The seeds should be at least 2in apart. Moringa thrives in moist soil and a little compost or manure.

- **Sprouting Seeds** *(Wheat, Barley, Alfalfa)*

Sprouting is a common practice among gardeners and farmers. This is done to preserve their nutrients. When seeds and grains are refined, many of their nutrients are stripped away. On the other hand, sprouting helps seeds retain their nutrients. It also makes them easier to digest and encourages them to grow good bacteria. There are three sprouting seeds that are must haves for victory gardens. These are:

1. Wheat - excellent for making quick breads and pastries.

2. Barley – needed to make syrup sweeteners and alcoholic beverages such as beer.

3. Alfalfa – best in sandwiches, salads and other dishes.

Sprouting seeds is as easy as cleaning them and submerging them in warm water overnight. In the morning, they are rinsed via a fine mesh sieve. The process is done for several days until they have sprouted enough.

Super seeds are excellent food sources for holistic care. They are filling, medicinal and at times ornamental. Although it may take some time and effort to grow and cultivate them, the benefits they provide far outweigh the initial sacrifices.

Here are some questions to see how much you've learned:

1. How many days will it take for Chia seeds to germinate?
2. How does Flaxseed help against cancer?
3. Is it possible to grow Moringa from branches? How?
4. What is the advantage of sprouted seeds over refined seeds?
5. Why are super seeds important for survival?

Here are the answers:

1. Chia seeds will germinate after four days so long as they are kept moist and covered.
2. Flaxseed contains high concentrations of Lignan which help against cancer.
3. Yes. Moringa branches, which are cut yearly, can be planted 3ft into the ground. Roots will grow from the branch in about two weeks.
4. Sprouted seeds retain the nutrients that are stripped away through refining.
5. Super seeds provide sustenance, nutrition and other practical benefits.

# 13. Creating Your Water World (Harvesting Water So You Can Harvest Your Crops)

Have you ever thought about where you'd get water when all your nearby water supplies run out of drops? Do you wish you could at least be self-reliant when it comes to the water you use or drink? There is one simple solution for this dilemma – create your own water world through a survivalist victory garden.

Why Water Independence Is Important

Water is essential for survival. In fact, the human body consists of almost three-fourths water, a significant loss of which can be fatal. This is why it is very important to make sure you never run out of water.

Water has many uses. It can be used for hydrating your system, cleaning your stuff, cooking, etc. Without it, life could become very difficult, if not unbearable.

The importance of water is such that you should never depend solely on some local water supply. They could run out of supplies, or they can just refuse to be of service. This might be unlikely, but there is always a risk you can't afford to take.

Creating Your Own Water World: 5 Things You Must Have

- **Rain Barrels**

    Having rain barrels in your victory survivalist garden is one way to store water in times of need. Rain barrels are large water containers usually made from wood that are used to store collected rain water. The rain water can be collected in two ways: 1) by having a waterway that leads to the rain barrels; 2) just leave the rain barrels open in an uncovered area so it could be filled with rain water.

In times of draught when water supply is limited, you could always make use of the rainwater you have stored during the rainy season. This will allow you to cut down on your water expenses as well as to help save limited water supply.

- **Ponds**

Having a pond in your garden is a good way not only to keep fishes in but is also a good way to ensure that you have some water to feed your plants come emergency time. However, take note that water from your garden pond can only be used as a water store for the plants. It should not be mistaken for human consumption. Water in a pond can already be contaminated or simply unclean. You can use this for flushing the toilet or cleaning your car though.

- **Swales**

A swale is a tract of land which is very low. It can either be a natural or an artificial one. Either way, swales can store up rainwater for future use.

Utilizing an artificial swale is one way for you to be water supply independent. If you want to, you may dig up on your backyard and form your own swale. The first thing that you have to do is to check the suitability of the land you're digging. Just make sure that the land your digging is moist enough to not absorb too much of your stored water; otherwise, you'll be left with none.

- **Wells**

Wells are very popular during the old times when water pipes and connections are not yet developed. In fact, this is a primary source of drinking water then.

Having a well in your garden can serve you in two ways: first, it can provide you with unlimited water supply; second, it has a very garden-like charm that increases your gardens appeal. What's not to love?

- **Local Lakes**

    Local lakes are another source of water supply. Most lakes are clean enough to supply you with your basic water needs such as plant watering, bathing, and cleaning, but you should always be cautious about using it for consumption. Again, make sure to apply the proper methods of water purifying first.

Purifying & Cleaning Water

There are a lot of options you can choose from if you decide to get your own water supply. But whichever option you choose to take, make sure that you undergo a series of cleaning and purifying your water before drinking it. There are a lot of pollutants that might infect the quality of your water, even though they are naturally sourced.

However, for purposes other than drinking, you can be more tolerant about water purification, especially if it only involves cleaning. Some of the means by which you can purify water is by boiling or by using a water filter.

Comprehension Questions

- Why do I need to have my own water world?

Water is very important for humans to survive. In fact, a human can only survive for three days without them. Because of this, it is imperative for you to be self-reliant when it comes to water supply. While it is good to have a local water supplier, it is better to be ready for any shortage.

- What are the advantages of having my own water supply?

There are a lot of benefits that you can get from having your own water supply. First, you will be finding more security with regard to meeting your water needs. Second, you'll get to cut on your water bills by using reserved water. Lastly, you'll be able to help conserve and maximize an otherwise limited resource.

- What are the things I need to start building a water world in the first place?

To start with your own water supply system, you need to get things settled first. There are many options for you; you can buy rain barrels and place it in your garden to collect and store rainwater or you may also dig up a well or a pond if you wish. The things you need to get your water system up and running depends on what method you choose.

- Is it safe to drink water from my own water supply?

It depends on the kind of water you are using. For example, if you are drinking from a well, make sure that your well is situated somewhere clean, or at least far away from harsh pollutants. But to be sure, purify and clean your water first before you drink it.

- Where else can I get water supply in case of emergency?

In case of emergency, you can get water supply from local lakes and swales.

# 14. The #1 Way To Naturally Eliminate Garden Pest (When Your Garden Thrives, You Can Survive)

Garden pests can really take a toll on the health of your plants. When they become uncontrollable, they can even destroy everything you've worked hard for. This is why you need to learn the basics of pest control.

There are a lot of pesticides available in the market nowadays. They can be effective in killing garden pests, but there is always the danger of chemical contamination, making it very risky. When pesticides infect the vegetables you eat, you risk being poisoned.

The good news is that you don't have to be on the losing side. You can protect your plants and still produce healthy and safe ones! How so? Use this wonder product: Diatomaceous Earth.

## What Is Diatomaceous Earth

Diatomaceous Earth is a naturally occurring substance which is classified as a siliceous sedimentary rock. It consists of fossil remains of hard-shelled algae called diatoms. This sedimentary rock is easily crumpled into a fine powder. It has many uses in agriculture, including that of being a natural pesticide. It is made up of three components: Silica (80-90 percent), alumina (2-4 percent) and iron oxide (.5- 2 percent).

## How Does Diatomaceous Earth Work

Diatomaceous Earth has so many uses; the most popular of which is its use in agriculture. Diatomaceous Earth works as a natural insecticide, and is often used by farmers for optimum pest control.

Unlike other insecticides, Diatomaceous Earth does not have any harmful effect. It works by physically eliminating the pests, and not by working its way chemically. Because of its composition, which is mainly silica, Diatomaceous Earth has a shard glass texture. Because of this, it is able to penetrate and puncture the body of the pests, hence killing them. It also dehydrates the pest it punctures, so it really has a double killing action.

## Using Diatomaceous Earth to Eliminate Bugs

Bugs can be very irritating, especially when it starts to crawl up to you at night. Bed bugs, in particular are very common, yet they are hard to get rid of. They could be anywhere near you, ready to pounce and suck your blood at every given opportunity.

Bed bugs are one of the most common bugs that interact with humans. They can be inside your closet, behind the sheets or in the cracks of your wallpaper. What is more dangerous is the fact that they can multiply fast, up to 5 eggs per day, and live up to 18 months. This is the reason why you have to act fast in killing them before they actually own your house. But how do you do that? Use Diatomaceous Earth.

To use this, you will need a plastic dispenser for sprinkling the Diatomaceous Earth powder and a powder duster for puffing the powder into walls and cracks.

What you should remember is that a bed bug can't fly. This would give you an easier time catching them with Diatomaceous Earth. Just put Diatomaceous Earth around your bed, into the creases and wherever you believe they walk on. This will leave them with no escape.

The good thing about this is that you won't have to move out while you do this. Diatomaceous Earth does not contain any chemical, so it is perfectly safe for you and your family.

Using Diatomaceous Earth For Pets & Animals

Pets and animals are the most common objects of parasites such as lice, tick, fleas and mites. This will not only cause endless itching on their part but it also has some health consequences. An animal so bugged with parasites will turn out to be weak and may eventually die.

The remedy for this is very simple – use Diatomaceous Earth. Diatomaceous Earth is safe for pets! All you have to do is to rub Diatomaceous Earth on their skin and on the ear flaps. This will surely kill present fleas as well as eggs and budding ones.

Since Diatomaceous Earth is a natural ingredient, it can be orally consumed by your pets. In fact, Diatomaceous Earth is an organic de-wormer. If you think your pet has worms, mix Diatomaceous Earth into their food. This will kill all the parasites inside their body without causing any harmful effect on your pet.

Using Diatomaceous Earth for Your Own Health

Being a natural product, Diatomaceous Earth can also be food grade. In fact, it has been so for years now and many people are claiming that they have experienced its benefits.

Food grade Diatomaceous Earth has been reported to absorb bad elements on the body. Some of them are:

- Methyl mercury
- Endotoxins
- Pesticide and drug residues
- E. Coli virus

For those who want to avail of the benefits of food grade Diatomaceous Earth, you can easily ingest it. It can be mixed with a juice or fruit shake and you have already taken it.

Here's a quick, powerful and rapidly effective way to have bugs vanish from your tender plants.

You will need some Diatomaceous Earth, Cayenne Pepper and a salt & pepper shaker.

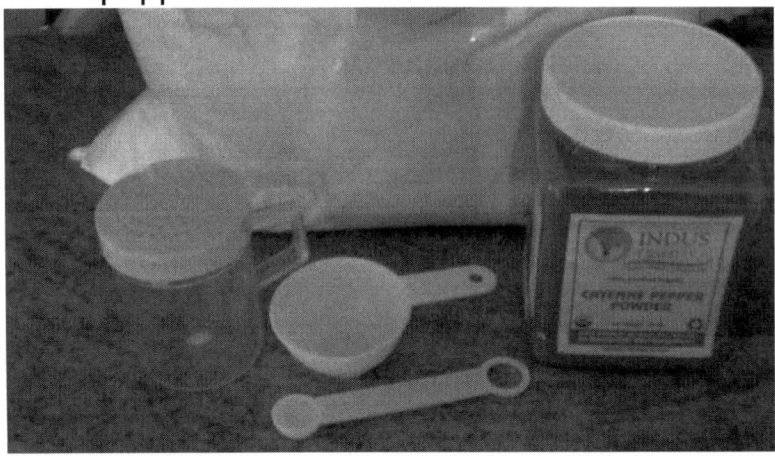

You want 1/2 cup of Diatomaceous Earth and 1 teaspoon Cayenne Pepper. (Shown below is 1/4 cup and 1/2 teaspoon so I just doubled up on them)

Put the Diatomaceous Earth into the salt and pepper shaker

Then add the Cayenne Pepper

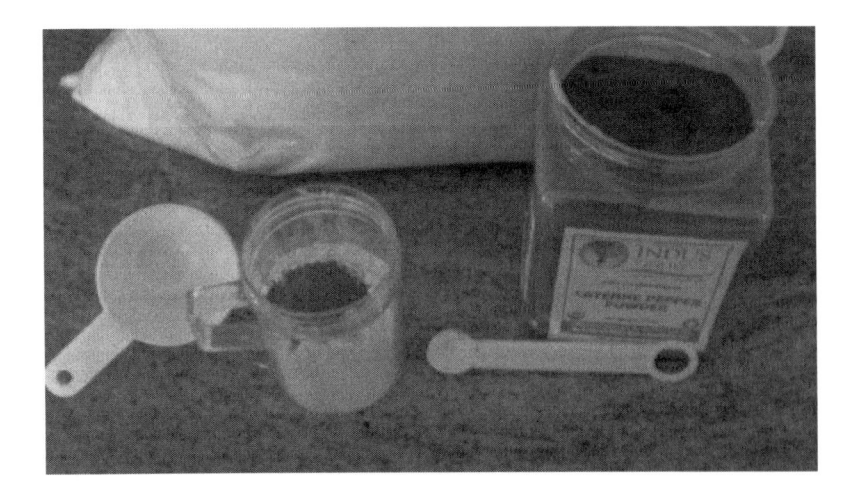

Now you want to mix the two together

Mix until completely blended

Put the top back on the shaker

Now you're ready to say "bye-bye bugs"

Simply shake the mixture on to your plants to give them an light dusting

And that's it. You're bugs be gone... gone... gone!

You can use this with fire ants, Hornworms that try to wreck your tomatoes and just about any bad bug.

The great thing is that this mixture does not harm or deter your beneficial insects.

Comprehension Questions

- Why is it important to implement pest control?

Pests, from the very word, are parasites. They will feed off you and this can have harmful consequences for you and for your pets. Moreover, pests have the ability to multiply fast. If you don't immediately implement pest control, you might just be too overwhelmed by them.

- What are the advantages of using Diatomaceous Earth

Diatomaceous Earth has many advantages. It is a naturally occurring substance, hence it is safe to use. Moreover, Diatomaceous Earth works to physically eliminate pests and it does not contain any chemical that can be harmful to both your health and the environment. While it is fatal to pests, Diatomaceous Earth is totally safe for humans and animals alike.

- How does Diatomaceous Earth work on pests?

Diatomaceous Earth works by physically puncturing the parasites because of its shard glass texture. After the pest has been punctured, Diatomaceous Earth works to dehydrate them. It kills the pests physically, unlike other pesticides which poison the pests so it would be killed.

- How does Diatomaceous Earth benefit your health?

Diatomaceous Earth can instantly boost your health by killing the parasites in your body. These parasites suck off your blood, as well as the nutrients contained in it. When you get rid of these parasites, you will be able to maximize the nutrients in your body.

- Is Diatomaceous Earth safe for humans?

Yes, Diatomaceous Earth is safe for humans. For human consumption though, you would need Diatomaceous Earth food grade. A food grade version is filtered and carefully processed to make sure that there is no harmful silica ingested.

# 15. More Pest Control Tips For YourGarden

There's nothing worse than working hard to create a beautiful garden only to have it destroyed by typical garden pests. Fortunately, with careful planning and care, you can prevent and treat common pest problems and enjoy your garden again.

No matter what type of garden you have, you'll be faced with pests that want to enjoy your bounty. Whether you're growing beautiful flowers to view or delicious garden vegetables, you should be prepared to defend your garden.

## Common Pests

The most common pests for gardens are all kinds of insects. There are thousands of different insects that might attack your garden looking for a free meal. But insects aren't the only ones who would like to enjoy your work.

Spiders, birds, mice, squirrels, and rabbits are also frequently found eating flowers and food from the garden. The way you handle your pest problem depends on what kind of pest it is.

You also have to deal with weeds that threaten to steal nutrients from your plants and overtake your garden. There's no garden free from the frustration of opportunistic weeds.

## Preventing Insect Infestation

There are many things you can do to prevent an insect infestation in your garden. The best defense is prevention. Make sure you think about this in the early stages of your garden so that you have fewer problems later.

Soil drainage is an important consideration. When soil is allowed to stay too wet for a long period of time, it creates conditions perfect for insect infestation. Insects enjoy a moist place to lay eggs and reproduce.

There are some plants that also keep insects away. Marigolds and basil are among the best choices for keeping your garden bug free. Insects tend to stay away from strong smelling herbs, so make sure you incorporate them into your garden.

Even if you don't want to grow a vegetable garden, planting herbs between flowering plants can prevent disease. And you get the added benefit of fresh herbs to use in your kitchen.

You can also introduce insects that are beneficial for your garden by allowing them to eat unwanted bugs. Ladybugs are a great introduction to your garden as they feed on aphids and help deter them from taking up residence in your space.

Adding coffee grounds to your soil can help your plants get more nutrients and can deter pests from your garden. Many bugs and animals dislike coffee. Most coffee shops are happy to give coffee grounds away to their customers for use in the garden.

Floating row covers are another method for preventing pests. This is a material that is white and allows light to come through it. You can cover plants with this material to keep insects out.

However, if the plants you're growing need pollination, a row cover can't be used for the entire growing season. These are especially good at preventing problems with cabbageworms, potato beetles, and aphids.

**Saying Goodbye to Invading Insects and Spiders**

If you're past the point of being able to prevent insects in your garden, you'll have to take more steps to get rid of them. If you prefer organic gardening, you can purchase insect-repelling sprays such as garlic or hot pepper spray.

You can also purchase organic pesticides that use organic materials to deter and kill pests. Many people think that organic gardening means not using pesticides. But many organic gardeners do use organic pesticides.

One common pesticide used in organic gardening is called Bt, which stands for Bacillus thuringiensis.

This is a bacteria that you can add to your garden that's harmless for plants, but harmful to insects. It comes in powder and liquid form and can really help eliminate insects that are destroying your plants.

Neem oil is another insecticide and also helps kill fungi and mites. It suffocates insects and acts as a repellent after they're gone. Neem oil also kills bees, so it's important to only use it sparingly.

Pyrethrins are another class of organic pesticide. This is a product made from chrysanthemum flowers. It's a broad spectrum product that works to fight many insects - including aphids, caterpillars, fleas, and fruit flies.

Using organic pesticides ensures that you won't pass on dangerous chemicals when you grow food. It also protects the environment from toxic chemicals that can make their way into the groundwater.

You can also choose pesticides made from synthetic chemicals. These are used by most commercial farms and end up in the food supply. Not much is understood about the result of pesticide exposure.

Many people feel that these are toxic to humans and can lead to health problems. If you choose to use pesticides for your garden, do it as safely as possible to ensure good health.

When you use pesticides in your garden, they don't stop there. They can end up in the air, water, and can make their way into your food. Use only synthetic pesticides that are deemed food safe if you're growing vegetables.

For flowers and ornamental plants, make sure that you don't come into contact with the pesticide. Wear gloves and a mask during application to make sure you don't inhale or come into contact with the chemical.

It's especially important that you keep children away from synthetic pesticides that could get into their system. And if you have pets, keep them out of any areas that contain pesticides to prevent illness and even death.

**Handling Larger Pest Problems**

There are other pests that can wreak havoc on your garden by eating your plants. Rabbits, deer, and squirrels are the greatest threats to the success of your garden.

Rabbits and squirrels may look cute – but when they start digging up your plants and eating the veggies in your garden, the cuteness fades. The only absolute way to prevent these little furry creatures from getting into your garden is to build a rodent-proof fence.

Having a barrier between your garden and the animals will keep them from eating your plants. But (especially if you have an ornamental garden) a fence doesn't always fit your needs.

You can spread bloodmeal around your garden to repel critters. Many animals associate the smell of blood with a predator, and bloodmeal is made from dried blood. Using it will cause animals to think twice before going in the garden.

You can also spray the garden with a solution of strong garlic and pepper that will taste bad to the animals if they taste it. Some people also use fox or coyote urine to repel animals.

Believe it or not, you can purchase this in bottles and sprinkle it in the garden.
Animals, even large animals such as deer, will be repelled by the smell because of their survival instincts.

If you're interested in a more high-tech solution, then you can use a motion sensor sprinkler. This will spray water when it senses motion from an animal. This is an effective and inexpensive way to deal with pests.

Deer are known for disliking strong, perfume smells. One way you can deter them is to place strong smelling soaps in your garden. The fragrance smells good to you, but causes deer to go another direction.

**Winning the Battle with Weeds**

Weeds are pests in their own right. They can take over an area of your garden and take nutrients from the plants you're trying to cultivate. But there are several things you can do to handle a weed problem.

One of the easiest things to do is to use a barrier between the soil and a layer of mulch. This blocks out the light source of weeds and keeps them from coming back. You can purchase special paper made for this purpose or use a material such as cardboard.

Pulling weeds when they're small is also a good way to keep them from getting out of control. You must make sure that you pull weeds from the root or they'll just grow right back.

While I <u>do not</u> recommend it, there are many products on the market that are designed to kill weeds and prevent them from growing. You can choose organic or synthetic products.

There are some natural ways to get rid of weeds that don't require harsh synthetic chemicals. One of the most effective is using horticultural vinegar. This is stronger than the vinegar you buy at the grocery store.

Spraying it directly on weeds will cause them to die. If you don't want to risk the spray hitting other plants, apply it to the leaves of the weeds with a paintbrush or sponge instead of spraying.

Pouring boiling water over weeds will also kill them. This is a great solution for weeds in a sidewalk or driveway.

## Creating Homemade Sprays and Traps for Pest Control

If you want to make your own safe and natural sprays, it's easy to do. You'll be able to create them easily with ingredients you may already have in your home. Here are a few different sprays and what they work against.

## Soap Spray

Probably the easiest spray to create at home is made from dish liquid. You can simply add a tablespoon of soap to a gallon of water. Pour it into a spray bottle and apply it to pests.

The soap spray will kill aphids and mites. It works by dissolving the outer shell of the insect, which is necessary for their survival.

## Hot Pepper Spray

A favorite among people gardeners who are trying to get rid of mites, hot pepper spray is easy to make. Simply add two tablespoons of hot pepper sauce, such as Tabasco, and a few drops of dish soap to one quart of water.

Let the spray sit overnight for the best effectiveness. This is a spray that irritates insects and causes them to keep away.

## Slug Trap

Slugs are common garden pests that threaten your plants. The best way to get rid of them is to trap them. You can create a simple trap by using a pie plate and a beer.

Simply place the pie plate on the ground in the area of the infestation. Pour enough beer to cover the sides of the pie plate about two inches. The slugs will be attracted to the beer and when they go to drink it, they'll get trapped.

You can also make a slug trap by using a large orange rind or grapefruit rind. Use about half of the rind of a fruit and invert it so that you have a bowl. Add a little water to the bottom. The slugs will be attracted to the citrus, and get trapped.

## Pests Can Be Things of the Past

While pests are a normal, natural part of growing a garden, you don't have to live in fear of them or just accept them as unwanted guests. These strategies will help you eliminate pests in the way that works best for you.

The more solutions you try, the more you'll learn about what will work best in your own garden. You may even find that you stumble upon even more methods that make pest control easier.

Whether you're growing a vegetable garden or a flower garden, finding the right pest control ensures a successful experience. When you keep pests out of the garden, you'll have more beautiful flowers and a more bountiful harvest.

# 16. Storing & Hoarding Your Harvest (So You Have No Need for the Store)

Basic Principles of Food Storage

The acronym HALT should always be put in mind when storing food. Following this acronym will help you store food properly, and avoid wasting money because of food spoilage.

1. Keep food away from HUMIDITY – food must always be stored on elevated platforms or shelves. Concrete walls and floors attract humidity, so placing food on these surfaces will make food susceptible to moisture damage.
2. Keep food away from AIR exposure.
3. Keep food away from sun LIGHT.
4. Keep food away from extreme TEMPERATURE. Ideal food storage temperature is between 40-60°F or cooler.

Consider the following factors before purchasing and storing food:

5. Make an inventory – don't just buy and store food. Take note of the food your household has consumed, and the food you just bought from the store.
6. Quality of food products – purchase high-quality products. If it's a BOGO deal, check the brand and expiration date beforebuying.
7. Suitable containers – use containers that are made of heavy plastic, glass, or metal with tight-fitting covers.
8. Incorporate variety – store foods from the different food groups to ensure a well-balanced diet.
9. Storage area – remember the acronym HALT. Make sure that your storage area is free

from pests like roaches, ants, flies, and rodents.
10. Rotation – first in first out.

Once you've got the hang of storing food, you may now try going without buying anything from the stores by relying on your harvests.

## Canning & Pickling

Pickling makes use of acid and salt to preserve food. There are 4 types of pickles namely:

11. Fermented/brined
12. Fruit
13. Relishes
14. Quick pack

Pickle relish
- Ingredients:
    o 3 quarts cucumbers; chopped
    o 3 cups sweet green peppers; chopped
    o 3 cups sweet red peppers; chopped
    o 1 cup of onion; chopped
    o ¾ cup pickling or canning salt
    o 2 cups of sugar
    o Water
    o Ice
    o 4 tsp. of each: Turmeric, mustard seed, whole cloves, and whole allspice
    o 6 cups of white vinegar

Procedure:

15. Prepare 2 batches of ice water – 4 cups of ice in 8 cups of water for each batch.
16. Add salt, cucumbers, onions, and peppers to ice water and let it stand for 4 hours. Drain the water and place the second batch of ice water over the vegetables. Let stand for another hour, then drain.

17. Place the spices in a spice bag. Get the saucepan and combine vinegar and sugar; place the spice bag in the pan. Heat the mixture until it boils. Pour it over the vegetables. Cover the mixture and refrigerate for 24 hours. Remove mixture from refrigeration and bring it to another boil. Get the clean jars and fill them with the hot relish and make sure to leave ½-inch allowance. Wipe the jar rims with a clean cloth. Adjust the lids and process in the boiling water canner for 10 minutes.

**Root Cellars & Cold Storage**

Root cellars are located in the basement and are good for storing fresh produce. A good root cellar has the following qualities:

18. Cool – before refrigerators came to be, people stored their produce in root cellars.
19. Humid – refrigerators tend to make produce dry and shrivel up. Fresh produce have to be stored in an area where there is an acceptable amount of humidity. Just watch out for molds on walls, this is an indication of high humidity.
20. Well-ventilated – make it in a way that air is able to recirculate around your house. Getting ventilation from outside can be risky because there is a tendency for warm air or high humidity to enter your basement.

**Dehydrated Food Storage**

Follow these 3 steps to store dehydrated food:

1. HALT – even if it is dried food, it is still susceptible to spoilage caused by the elements.
2. Dried food should be consumed within six to twelve months.
3. Check dried foods to see if there is moisture in the packaging. The tiniest amount of moisture can cause molds to

grow on your food.

## Mylar Pouches with Oxygen Absorbing Packets

Mylar pouches are a vital component of food storage systems. These food-grade metalized bags are the ones that line food storage containers. Mylar pouches prevent oxygen from coming into contact with food to extend shelf-life.

Oxygen absorbing packets are seen in most food packaging. These little packets remove oxygen from the packaging, allowing food to be stored long-term. Oxygen absorbers also prevent aerobic pathogens and molds from growing on food.

It is not necessary to purchase Mylar pouches and put oxygen absorbing packets in them, because both of them do the same job. If you have Mylar pouches and oxygen absorbing packets on hand, you might want to think of other uses for them e.g. Mylar pouches can be used as storage for seeds.

## 5 Gallon - Food Grade - BPA Free Plastic Buckets With Oxygen Absorbing Packets

Before purchasing a food bucket, make sure that it is FDA-approved food grade plastic, and BPA free. Check the lid and see if it has a food grade rubber gasket. The rubber gasket will ensure that your bucket will be airtight and free from any pest infestation. If you're going to store grains in these buckets, place one oxygen absorbing packet for each 5-gallon bucket. Once you've consumed the contents of the bucket, dispose of the oxygen absorbing packet. Those are meant for single-use only.

## Storing your Coleman 58-Quart Ultimate Extreme Marine Cooler in a 4-Foot Dug Hole in the Ground

The Coleman 58-Quart Ultimate Extreme Marine Cooler can keep your food and drinks cold for approximately a week. Its insulation can hold the cold for six days even in temperatures that reach up to 90°F. You can increase its insulation by burying it in a 4-foot hole in the ground.

Questions:

1. What does HALT stand for?
2. It is a food preservation process that makes use of vinegar and salt.
3. Dried food can spoil even with the smallest amount of _____.
4. _____ and _____ may be used to prevent oxygen from entering food containers.
5. Should you place stored food on concrete floors, or near concrete walls? If no, why?

Answers:

1. Humidity, Air, Light, Temperature
2. Pickling
3. Moisture
4. Mylar pouches and oxygen absorbing packets

No. Concrete attracts humidity. Foods that are stored on concrete surfaces will be exposed to moisture. Moisture can cause molds to grow on food.

# 17. Saving Seeds for Sustainable Gardening (Building Your Own Seed Bank)

In the previous articles, you have been taught about the importance of growing and maintaining your own victory garden. This article will be about the types of seed processing, seed storage, and the importance of keeping notes about your seeds.

### 3-Step Wet Processing

Wet processing of seeds is used for seeds that come from fleshy fruits.

1. Seed extraction

Fruits like melons and tomatoes are sliced in half, their flesh and seeds are scraped out, and are stored in a container to ferment. Fermentation is done to kill off any fungi and bacteria responsible for common seed-borne diseases. Fermentation depends on the surroundings' temperature and the variety of the fruit. Fruits that are high in sugar usually take 3-4 days to ferment, while fruits that are low in sugar typically take a day or two to ferment.

2. Cleaning the seeds

After the fermentation process, you have to wash the seeds to remove pieces of fruit, remaining fruit fibers, and low-quality seeds

3. Drying the seeds

After washing, make sure to dry the seeds fairly quickly. Seeds that are dried in a slow manner will usually result in untimely sprouting of the seed or mold growth. Dark-colored seeds shouldn't be left out too long since they absorb more sunlight than light-colored ones.

Here is a sample on how to do wet processing:
Materials needed for seed extraction for fleshy fruits:
- knife
- clean container or cup
- two tablespoons of clean water
- paper towel to cover the container
- kitchen strainer or wire mesh sieve
- Paper towel
- spoon
- non-stick surface to put the seeds on

Slice the fruit and scoop out the fleshy part with the seeds and mash them together gently. You don't want to crush the seeds. Place the mashed fruit along with 2 tablespoons of water into a container. Cover the container with a paper towel. Puncture tiny holes on the paper towel – preferably with a needle – to allow air to get in and out of the container to aid the fermentation process.

Clean the seeds thoroughly after the fermentation process by removing the pulp and other debris from the container. After removing the pulp, place the seeds into the sieve and wash them under running water. This will further remove remaining debris. Place the clean seeds into a container with water. Stir and remove the seeds that will float to the surface.

Spread the good seeds in a thin and even manner onto a non-stick surface. Never line the surface with cloth or any paper. The seeds will stick to it and will be hard to remove. Make sure that the seeds get enough sun. Stir the seeds from time to time to dry them thoroughly. When the sun goes down, you may bring the seeds inside the house. Once they feel dry, you may store them.

**Dry Processing**

Capsules, pods, or seed heads become brown and dry when they are ready for processing. Sometimes, ripening and maturation is uneven within the seedpod, so seedpod harvesting is usually done individually. Brassicas and legumes are best harvested when a spilt occurs along its pod. After harvest, the seeds are ready to be threshed. Threshing is done to remove any material sticking onto the seeds. Seeds can be threshed by placing the pods in a sack, tied securely, and laid on the soil where it is jogged on, or flailed. Make sure to wear running shoes to prevent the seeds from cracking.

**Hot Water Treatment**

Hot water treatment can prevent bacterial diseases and black rot on vegetable crops and cole crops respectively. Hot water is able to penetrate seeds and kill off bacteria and fungi, unlike chemicals. Tomato seeds are heated for 2 minutes at 125 °F, pepper and cabbage seeds for 25 minutes at 122 °F, and cauliflower seeds for 20 minutes at 122 °F.

Materials needed for hot water treatment:

- laboratory thermometer
- stirring hot plate
- cheesecloth
- sinker

A laboratory thermometer and stirring hot plate are needed to provide an accurate and even water temperature. Wrap the seeds in cheesecloth and add a sinker to keep the seeds submerged. Bring the water to the appropriate temperature for the seed you're treating. Remove the seeds after the recommended heating time, cool them under tap water, and dry them by spreading them evenly on a non-stick surface.

## Storing Seeds in Mylar Pouches

According to some experts, seeds stored in Mylar pouches can last a decade or two. Seed longevity depends on seed variety, how it was harvested, and where it is stored. Seeds kept frozen can last for two decades.

## Storing Seeds Using Airtight Storage Containers

Desiccation-tolerant seeds like garden produce are all right to be kept in airtight storage containers; provided that they have been dried thoroughly before storage.

## Long-Term Frozen Seed Storage

Seeds can be stored long-term if they are dried properly, kept from oxygen and high humidity, and stored in a cool or frozen environment. Just put them in a Mylar pouch or a seed packet and store in a cool or frozen storage. Once you take the seeds from their storage, you have to plant them immediately.

## 7 Important Seeds Notes for Record Keeping

You don't have to be a farmer to keep a record of your seeds and crops. Record keeping is important so that you won't have a hard time identifying the (1) type and (2) variety of plant the seeds are coming from. Keep tabs on the (3) date of last season when that crop has grown, so that you'll have an idea on how much that crop will yield the following season. Plant seeds that were processed and stored earlier; that's why it's important to take note when (4) the seeds were saved. (5) Germination percentage will indicate how much seed you will need for future planting. Take note of any important events like pests or crop yield during (6) the harvest where the seeds came from. Finally, make sure to keep a (7) detailed seed history and variety to know which seeds are viable to store and plant.

Questions:

1. Name the steps involved in wet processing.
2. In dry processing,_____is done to remove any material sticking onto the seeds.
3. What is the importance of hot water treatment?
4. True or False. Dark-colored seeds should be left out under the sun for a long time. If true, why?
5. Why should you keep a detailed seed history and variety?

Answers:

1. Seed extraction, cleaning the seeds, and drying the seeds
2. Threshing
3. Hot water treatment kills off any bacteria and fungi inside the seeds. It is better than chemical treatments, because hot water can penetrate the seeds thoroughly.
4. False
5. It will help me identify which seeds are viable to store and plant.

# 18. Shooting Fish in a Barrel (Growing Tilapia in Barrel or IBC Aquaponics)

## History of Aquaponics

The history of Aquaponics can be traced back in Central America in the early 1000s. The Aztec Indians used to be a nomadic tribe that settled near the swamps of Lake Tenochtitlan. They had fish but they couldn't grow crops because they were surrounded by hills and swamps. In order to grow crops, they thought of an ingenious way to plant crops without having to search far and wide for dry land.

The Aztecs collected large reeds and constructed them into large rafts. They dredged up soil from the shallow lake's bottom and covered the rafts with it. The rafts were named by the Aztecs as chinampas. The Aztecs planted various crops like squash and maize onto the chinampas. The chinampas were allowed to float on the lake, and when the plants developed, their roots pierced through the dirt and dangled beneath the raft. Fish excrement served as fertilizer for the plants.

Other records state that Thailand and China were the first East Asian countries to utilize Aquaponics. Farmers cultivated rice and grew fishes in paddies – the fishes got rid of rice parasites while providing fertilizer for the crops.

Today, Aquaponics is still being developed in different countries worldwide. Agriculturists are also developing an effective Aquaponics system that will aid third world countries in arid regions to grow their own food, and to become less dependent on expensive importation.

## How Does Aquaponics Work?

Aquaponics is a natural process that mimics an actual ecosystem without having to use any chemical additives. Aquaponics comes from the words "Aquaculture" and "hydroponics". The three main components of an Aquaponic system are plants, fish, and microbes. Some Aquaponics systems use alternative cultivating media like gravel, clay pebbles, lava rock, pumice stone, or the plants are simply suspended in a separate water tank nourished by the nutrients coming from an adjoining fish tank.

The ammonia coming from fish waste becomes harmful in elevated quantities. This is where the microbes come in. The naturally-occurring microbes from the plant grow bed break down ammonia into nitrite then nitrate. Nitrate is absorbed by the plants, and in the process, the water gets cleaned. Water quality is improved afterwards. The plants take in nitrate while giving off oxygen that the fish need.

**The Big Benefits of Aquaponics**

- You can harvest crops and fish

The fish provide the plants nutrients, and the plants provide oxygen for the fish.

- Low water consumption

Water in an Aquaponics system is only lost by being taken up by the plants or evaporation; unlike in soil planting where water is lost due to run off.

- All natural

Once again, the three main components of an Aquaponic system are plants, fish, and microbes. The only thing you have to add in the system is fish food. Pesticides aren't used because there is no soil for the pests to hide in.

- Fresh produce

Tired of paying for hidden, wilted leafy-greens? You won't get those with Aquaponics.

· Raise edible fish

Survivalists need all the nutrition they can get. Now you can get vitamins from your crops, and protein from fish.

· Low maintenance

Daily maintenance won't eat up half of your day.

## Types of Aquaponic Systems

· Deep Water Culture

Plants are allowed to float on top of the water while their roots dangle below the water. Some people use foam rafts to suspend plants right above the fish tanks, while the most common method makes use of separate tanks where water from the fish tank is pumped along a channel going to the tank with plants.

· Nutrient Film Technique

This is a technique commonly used in hydroponics wherein water rich in nutrients is pumped through small enclosed channels. The plants are placed in small cups where their roots dangle in the water beneath them. NFT is only suitable for leafy-greens, because their roots are thin and small.

· Media Filled Beds

This is the simplest and most common Aquaponics system. The containers used in the system are filled with rock medium. This system can either be run by flooding and draining the grow bed, or by providing a continuous flow of water over the medium. The water drained from the medium bed is recycled via a pump.

## How to Get Started With Aquaponics

As a survivalist getting ready for anything, you have to consider the viability of your food sources. Raising tilapia is the best choice of fish for your system, because they are easy to maintain. They breathe air, unlike other fish that suffocate when a tank gets quite crowded. Tilapias are herbivorous, thus feeding them vegetable scraps is fine. The only downsides to raising tilapias are they are prone to overpopulating, and being tropical fish, they require warm water to survive.

If this is your first time to try your hand at Aquaponics, you might want to start with produce like lettuce and tomatoes, because they are small and easy to grow.

Here are the usual materials needed for a basic Aquaponics system:

- 2 Food-grade bins/barrels – one to contain the grow bed and plants, and the other one is for the fish tank.
- Conventional power tools
- A Pump for the flood and drain system
- Medium for the grow bed
- Clean tap water
- Air bubbler to remove other impurities in the water
- Sturdy plank to put on top of the tilapia container. This is where you'll be putting your plant bin on later.

Installation:

- Before putting the tilapia in the container, make sure to age the tap water for a day or two and run the air bubbler to further clean the water.
- Drill a hole underneath the plant bin, and put the medium in it. The medium should not be too compact or too loose. Check if water can still seep through the hole.
- Put the pump into the tilapia container, and connect its hose to the plant bin. Turn the pump on to activate your Aquaponics

system.
- Make sure to cycle your system to build up the beneficial bacteria.
- Once the system is cycled you can start planting your produce.

Please note that this Aquaponics system is for home-use only. Commercial systems are larger and more complex than this.

Questions:

b. Aquaponics came from the words _____ and _____.
c. Name the 3 types of Aquaponics system.
d. True or False. Aquaponics makes use of soil medium. If yes, why?
e. What are the downsides with raising tilapia?
f. What are the 3 main components of an Aquaponics system?

Answers:

1. Aquaculture and hydroponics
2. Deep Water Culture, Nutrient Film Technique, and Medium Filled Beds
3. False
4. Tilapias are prone to overpopulating, and they need warm water to thrive.
5. Plants, fish, and microbes.

## HIGHLY RECOMMENDED READING

Aquaponic Gardening: A Step-By-Step Guide to Raising Vegetables and Fish Together

## The Aquaponics Answers Book - How To Raise Tilapia & Grow Tasty Vegetables

# 19. Reasons to Grow Your Own Victory Garden

Growing your very own Victory Garden can be a great idea to spend your spare time. This enables you to have a lower expense on food because you already have your own supply of vegetables.

You also enjoy less risk of pesticide contamination if you don't use it to grow your produce. Moreover, a Victory Gardens allows you to have an activity you can do with your family and friends during your spare time. There are definitely more reasons why growing a Victory Garden in your backyard (or front yard) is a great idea and here are more of them:

*Fresher Produce*

If you grow your own vegetables, you are sure that your produce is always fresh. There is no need for transportation just to get your supply of vegetables. You can simply pick one up in your backyard and take it directly to your kitchen. There is no more waiting time just to get your supply of vegetables from the farmland to the market to your kitchen.

The thing with most modern farms today is that you can never be too sure if their produce is fresh or not. With the continuous development of technology in farming, there are now ways to preserve produce that were not employed before. This way, farmers save on transportation costs. But in the end, it is the consumers who will suffer because of too much preservatives present on the vegetables they consume.

This is why a Victory Garden is a great thing to have in your backyard. You don't have to use preservatives just to make sure that the vegetables will reach your kitchen in good condition. Therefore, you get nothing but the freshest produce that is healthy and good for your body.

*Healthier Produce*

In line with the aforementioned reason to convert your backyard into a Victory Garden is that since your produce is fresh, you can be sure that it is healthy. You control your own backyard and you get to decide what to use to grow your crops and what not to use. Therefore, you have control whether to use pesticides or not, and whether or not to use organic fertilizers or chemical fertilizers.

Most farmers today use pesticides and chemical fertilizers intensively that will not only damage the land but the vegetables they produce as well. Hence, most vegetables we can find sold in the market today can be potentially detrimental to our health. But if you grow your own vegetables, you have the option of going organic to make your produce healthier.

You can make your own fertilizers by creating a compost pit in your home to make your land more nutritious for your vegetables. You can also opt to not use pesticides to make your produce healthier. With a Victory Garden at home, you consume only the healthiest crops that do not contain any trace of pesticides or chemical fertilizers.

*Cheaper than Buying in the Market*

Clearly, one of the major reasons you will want a Victory Garden at home is because it is cheaper than constantly buying vegetables in the market. Consider how much you spend each week in the market for vegetables and compare it to how much you will spend buying seeds to plant your own vegetables in your Victory Garden. While it is true that planting and growing your own vegetables may be labor intensive and time consuming, you get to save more money in the end.

Besides, you don't have to attend to your vegetables all the time anyway. You just have to plow the soil and put some fertilizers, plant the seeds, water the soil every day and leave it there to grow. And then after a few weeks, harvest your vegetables. Also, you get to use your idle time in a productive way by planting and growing your own vegetables so you never have a dreary time when you have nothing to do. Not only does growing a Victory Garden help you save money, it also saves you from a dreary moment.

*Feeling of Security*

With the continuous rise and fall of the economy, one may feel insecure about the food supply and prices of commodities in the market. One day, everything is so cheap and the next day everything is too expensive. With this kind of trend, you can never be too sure if there is enough supply of vegetables in the market and you can never be too sure if the prices are affordable.

This then makes growing your own Victory Gardens valuable. If you have one, you can always be secured that you have a constant supply of vegetables and that they are free. You never have to worry about the fluctuating prices of vegetables in the market because you never have to pay for it anyway. You can always get one from your backyard for free. Growing a Victory Garden can make anyone feel secure no matter the economic situation.

*Organic Produce*

You have the option to grow your crops organically to make them healthier. As aforementioned, you have the option not to use pesticides and chemical fertilizers. Since you only have a small piece of land for your produce, it won't be too hard to continuously monitor your crops for pests and to use organic fertilizers to make the soil more nutritious for a healthier and better result. By going organic with your produce, you get better and healthier results.

A Victory Garden has helped a lot of people during the war years and was able to feed a lot of hungry people back then. Today, the campaign is being re-launched and idle lands are slowly being converted to Victory Gardens again. This movement can help create a healthier and more self sufficient nation that can withstand any economic crisis.

Do you want fresher vegetables on your plate? Do you want to eat healthy and become healthier? Do you want to save more money from constantly buying food in the market? Do you want to stay secure and not be affected by economic crisis? Do you want organic produce that will keep you healthy? If you say yes to all of these questions, then growing a Victory Garden is a great option for you.

# 20. Tower Gardening Questions and Answers

Tower gardening is the latest trend that allows people to grow their own food at home. If you've wanted to grow your own fresh produce, but you don't have a large yard, this is the answer you've been looking for.

## What Is a Tower Garden?

A tower garden is a type of vertical garden, but you use it to grow food aeroponically. That means that you grow without soil using only air and water to grow your plants.

You can grow a large variety of plants vertically - saving space. You can grow your tower garden on a roof, patio, or balcony without having to haul heavy soil. Even if you have a yard, you can save space by growing a tower garden.

Tower gardens are also attractive and can provide you with a functional way to beautify a small space.

With the price of produce rising and the safety of many commercial farms a concern, a tower garden is an investment that will pay off. This is perfect for the gardener who's interested in producing organic food for his family.

## The Benefits of a Tower Garden

There's obviously a benefit of being able to grow food in a small space with a tower garden. However, it has many other benefits when it comes to gardening. If you've ever grown food in soil, you'll appreciate the ease of a tower garden.

When growing without soil, you can eliminate most garden pests. Without soil, most insects that would attack your plants are not an issue. You may occasionally have to deal with some insects, but it will be on a much smaller scale.

Weeding is another task that's much less of a chore when you have a tower garden. It's not impossible for weeds to find their way to your garden, but you'll find that there are fewer than you would have in a traditional garden.

Because you're growing vertically, you'll also have less bending and stooping than you would have when working with a typical garden bed. This is especially helpful if you have back or knee problems that make gardening difficult.

This is also a cost effective way to grow your own food. You'll have to make an initial investment in equipment to grow your garden, but you won't have to spend much after that. And the money you'll save on produce will more than pay for the cost of the garden.

And another added benefit of tower gardening is that your food will grow to maturity in less time than it would in soil. That's less time for you to wait before you can begin enjoying the fruits of your labors.

**How Does a Tower Garden Work?**

A tower garden is made of a large plastic column that has hydroponic net pots placed throughout it. Internally, a pump keeps water moving over the roots of the plants that you grow.

The tower garden also has a reservoir that contains a liquid fertilizer that helps plants get the nutrients they need so that they can continue to grow. You'll still need to make sure your plants get plenty of sunlight so that they can thrive.

When you purchase a tower garden kit, you have to put it together. The process is simple and easy and usually takes about a half hour. You'll have to grow your seedlings separately, but tower gardens come with a seed starting kit to help you with that part of it.

Once you have seedlings that are mature enough to be transplanted, you can add them to your tower garden. After that, you'll have to perform some routine maintenance to care for your plants.

You'll need to test the water in your tower garden to make sure the pH is correct. You'll also need to clean the filter that keeps debris out of the pump. You'll also need to make sure you don't have any weeds or insect problems, though these are rare.

In a few weeks you'll be able to harvest vegetables and greens from your garden that you can use right away in your kitchen. Fresh produce will just be a few steps from your back door.

**The Cost of a Tower Garden**

At this time, there's one manufacturer of the official tower garden where you can purchase this system. One tower that includes everything you need to get started, including seeds, will cost you around $500.

This tower will give you the space to grow up to 20 different plants. You can also purchase an extension that allows you to plant up to 28 different plants. Starting with one tower is a great way to get started.

But if you have a large family and cook frequently, you may want more than one tower. If you purchase the Tower Garden Family Garden package, you'll save money by purchasing three towers at once.

You can also purchase supplies separately if you need accessories or replacement items. You can also purchase a heater if you live in a cold climate so that you can still grow in cooler temperatures.

Many people wonder if the garden is worth the upfront costs. If you've been to the supermarket lately, you know how much it costs to feed you family fresh produce.

While you'll have to spend money up front with this system, you'll save much more than you spend by not having to purchase produce at the market.

**What Can I Grow with a Tower Garden?**

You may be wondering if a tower garden will really provide you with the types of foods your family eats. The good news is that a tower garden allows you to grow a wide variety of foods.

You can grow vegetables such as broccoli, cauliflower, cucumbers, eggplant, endive, lettuce, peas, and spinach. You can also grow tomatoes, strawberries, and melons to add sweetness to your garden.

If you love to use fresh herbs, a tower garden can help you enjoy your favorites. When you grow them yourself you get the freshest flavor. Herbs you can grow include basil, chives, cilantro, cumin, dill, lavender, oregano, parsley, sage, and thyme. But you can grow almost any herb.

And if you prefer to grow flowers, or you just want to place a few different flowers in your vegetable garden, there are many flowers that grow well. Some of the most successful varieties are marigolds, salvia, pansies, and sunflowers.

If you love gardening, you'll be happy to know that you can grow almost anything you would grow in a traditional garden using less space and fewer natural resources. You'll also get a large crop in less time.

**Is Tower Gardening Organic?**

Most people who grow their own vegetables are interested in the practice of organic gardening because they want to avoid harmful chemicals including fertilizers and pesticides.

Tower gardening is not technically considered organic gardening because it doesn't use soil – and that's a key principle of organic gardening. However, you can eliminate the need for herbicides and pesticides by using this garden.

You will have to add a fertilizer solution to the plant roots because they won't be in soil to get nutrients. Because this type of gardening takes less space and fewer natural resources than traditional gardening, it's a good alternative that's eco-friendly and safe for your family.

## How Will Produce Taste from a Tower Garden?

If you've never had fresh food from a garden, you'll be surprised when you take your first bite of something you've grown. By the time your local supermarket gets the produce grown commercially, it's been picked for days, weeks, and even months.

Food is often harvested before it's truly ripened to extend its shelf life. When you eat food from your garden at home, you can pick it when the food is really ripe and you're able to experience a new level of flavor.

If you enjoy specific flavors in vegetables or fruits, you'll find those flavors are magnified when you eat homegrown produce. Tomatoes will be sweeter, peppers will have more intense layers of flavor and berries will be juicer.

Once you've tasted produce from your own tower garden, you'll never be satisfied with produce from the grocery store again. If you grow more food than you can eat in a short time, you can freeze, can, or dry it in order to preserve those fresh flavors.

## Is the Plastic in a Tower Garden Safe?

One of the greatest concerns people have with the idea of a tower garden is that it's made from plastic. As you may already know, plastic can leach chemicals into surrounding water and soil if gets heated.

Naturally, you don't want your food to contain extra chemicals that are dangerous or can cause illness. The good news is that this type of garden is treated with a UV protector that helps keep the plastic from breaking down.

You can rest assured that your garden will grow healthy produce unaffected by chemicals that leach from the plastic because of this protection. The plastic also helps keep the roots of your plants cool and prevents the growth of algae.

**Can Children Enjoy a Tower Garden?**

One of the best ways you can entice children to eat healthy foods is to allow them to have a role in growing it. Tower gardens are wonderful ways to introduce children to the world of food production.

Many kids who grow up in urban areas have no idea where food really comes from. They simply see it at the store and some even believe that it's made in factories.

A tower garden is perfect for urban areas to give kids who live in a city the ability to see how food is grown and to enjoy the process. It's a good idea to let kids choose some different varieties to grow and watch what happens.

This is a great way to bring healthier foods to your table and give your children an education about safe and environmentally responsible food production.

**Tower Gardening Is Healthy Gardening**

Now that you understand some basics about a tower garden, it's important to also understand the health benefits for you and your family. Many people don't consume enough fruits and vegetables. This is sometimes because of the cost, but it's also about the flavor.

When you grow your own food, you'll be saving money and you'll have foods that are better in flavor. You'll spend less time and energy on grocery shopping and more time enjoying food that grows outside your back door.

You'll also be able to enjoy food that's free from toxins. Many researchers suggest that pesticides, herbicides, and chemical fertilizers can cause problems with inflammation, weight gain, cancer, and auto-immune diseases.

When you grow your own food, you can eliminate anything that you don't feel is safe. The fertilizer used for this system comes from minerals, rather than harsh chemicals that can be dangerous.

The time that it takes food to travel from a large farm to a grocery store produce section is time for the nutrition to dwindle. When you eat fresh food from your garden, you're getting more vitamins and minerals than supermarket produce provides.

You may have thought you could never have a garden because of limited space or the inability to bring in soil, but a tower garden makes it possible to have a garden in any area that receives sunlight. You can also add a grow light if your patio doesn't get at least four hours of sun each day.

A tower garden is a cost effective way to enjoy fresh produce throughout the year. You'll enjoy the ease of use, the speed of growth, the fresh flavor and the nutritional quality of the foods you eat.

# 21. Container Victory Gardening

The first thing you need to decide when planning a container garden is whether you'd prefer to grow your plants indoors or outdoors. A lot of people think container gardening is only for indoor growing and patios, but containers can actually be useful for any garden situation.

Containers are great for growing almost any type of plant, because they offer great versatility. If you plant your garden in containers and you need to move it later, it's easy to do it. Not so if you have a traditional garden!

If you're expecting very bad weather, you can temporarily move containers to a safer location, like indoors or into a garage or basement. But there isn't much you can do for a traditional garden.

If you find your plants aren't doing well because the space you chose is too sunny or too shady, there isn't much you can do with a traditional garden, but you can easily move potted plants to a better location.

If you choose to have your container garden outdoors, you need to be sure to choose a good location for it. You'll want to choose a place that has the proper amount of sun for the plants you wish to grow, but it also needs to be a place that's very accessible. It's easy to lose motivation to work on your garden if it's several hundred yards away from the house!

Be sure to locate your plants as far away from streets as you can. Pollution from cars, as well as the dust they kick up, can damage your plants and contaminate them. You don't want to be eating all of that pollution, so locate plants as far away from those roads as possible.

If you have your plants indoors, you'll need to be sure to select a very good spot. Most plants need to be fairly warm, so you'll need to choose the warmest spot in your house if you use air conditioning.

Many plants won't do well in very chilly homes, so you might need to choose a room for your plants and keep the vent closed in that room so it stays warmer there. If you can, choose a sunny room with a lot of natural sunlight.

Plants thrive best with natural light. If you don't have a room with a lot of sunlight, you'll have to use special plant lights for your plants. You can't use just any fluorescent lights, because plants won't thrive.

You need to use lights that are specially designed for growing plants. They contain a broad spectrum of light, which is closer to natural light than standard bulbs. You may also have to adjust the humidity in the room with your plants.

Some plants thrive better in higher humidity, and others do well in lower humidity. You may need to invest in special equipment to adjust the humidity if you're raising very delicate or picky plants. You probably won't have to do this unless you're growing exotic varieties.

Next, you'll need to choose which plants you want to grow. Be careful! Too many people choose to plant far too many varieties, and end up frustrated. Don't grow anything you can easily pick up cheaply at the grocery store!

Stick to growing fruits and vegetables that you really enjoy and have a hard time locating locally, or those you find too expensive or too low quality. Tomatoes are a favorite for home gardeners, because their quality in stores if often very poor.

Finally, decide whether or not you want to grow your plants organically. If you're growing indoors, this will probably be very simple to do. But if you're growing your plants outside, you may find the frustration of dealing with pests is just too much for you. Don't feel guilty if you find organic gardening too difficult. You can always try it after you have more experience.

**Choosing Containers for Your Container Victory Garden**

Choosing the right container for a particular type of plant is critical to its success. If you choose the wrong size pot, it could seriously stunt the growth of the plant. You need to choose the right size of pot, but it's almost as important to choose a container that's made of the right material. Different materials will work better in different situations.

If you're planning to grow a perennial plant, like a large herb bush, you might want to choose a large wooden container. Wood is especially attractive for use in growing plants that will continue growing for more than one season, and plants that you intend to grow outdoors in a conspicuous location.

Wooden containers are best for larger plants, and for use in highly visible areas of your yard. Wooden pots are generally one of the most expensive types of containers. Wooden pots may be expensive, but they're generally extremely durable.

Be sure to get one that's treated on the outside, but not on the inside. If you get a pot that's treated on the inside, you might end up with dangerous chemicals being leeched into the soil and making their way into your plants. This can damage the plants, and potentially make you sick if you eat them.

Plastic pots are probably the most widely used type of pot for container gardening. This is largely due to the fact that plastic pots are generally the cheapest. But cheaper isn't always better.

If you only plant to attempt container gardening for one year, then plastic may be a very good option for you. But if you think you might want to have a container garden next year, you might want to stick with something a bit more durable.

You could be tempted to think certain plastic pots are durable because they're harder or thicker than other plastic pots, but that's not necessarily true. If plastic is left outdoors in the elements for too long, it can start to warp and crack. Cracked pots are of little use for anything!

Terra cotta clay pots are the second most economical type of container. They're pretty cheap, but they are very delicate and do break quite easily. They also don't stand up very well to freezing temperatures, so you shouldn't leave them out during the winter.

Fired ceramic pots are a pretty good choice. They can be a bit delicate, but many of them are pretty durable. They're usually glazed on the outside for appearance, but are left unglazed on the inside. This is good since the glaze can damage plants if it leeches into the soil.

You can also make your own containers by using things you find around the house. Most cheap plastic containers can work if they're large enough for whatever you want to grow, as long as you cut drainage holes in the bottom.

Some good example you can try are milk jugs and soda bottles with the tops cut off and holes cut in the bottom, empty margarine tubs, trash cans with holes cut in the bottom, and large plastic tubs with drainage holes drilled.

Some people even use bags of soil as their containers, simply cutting a hole in the side of a bag of soil that's lying on its side and sowing seeds directly into the exposed soil! You don't have to use standard purchased containers. Almost any container can be used for growing plants as long as it is safe and allows the plants adequate drainage.

**Choosing Plants for Your Container Victory Garden**

Most people choose to grow edible plants in their container gardens, because they don't think of flowers or houseplants as being the same thing as container gardening. While it is the same basic principle, it's not generally classified the same way.

Most people just think the term container gardening refers to growing edible plants, so that's what we'll focus on here. You can grow many types of vegetables and herbs in containers, and a few types of fruit.

Herbs are the most commonly grown edible plant for containers. Vegetables come in second, and fruit isn't grown in containers as often - probably because a lot of people think it would be too difficult to grow fruit in containers.

Strawberries are one fruit that grows particularly well in many types of containers. Strawberries are generally quite hardy, and can even be grown in special grow bags that can be hung on a wall outdoors.

Dwarf fruit trees can often be grown in large pots. Many smaller dwarf citrus trees grow nicely in pots, and if kept well-pruned they can make beautiful indoor decorations. Many types of dwarf berry bushes will grow in containers, although they are usually very heavy and can't be moved easily. Dwarf varieties of blueberries and raspberries have been successfully grown in containers.

Many varieties of herbs do well in containers. Parsley is perhaps the most popular herb for container growing. Basil and chives are also extremely popular for growing in containers. Cilantro can be grown successfully in containers.

In fact, almost all herbs can be grown successfully in containers. The key is finding a large enough container. Some herbs can easily be grown in relatively small containers. Chives, parsley, and basil can all grow in smaller pots.

But some plants grow a bit larger. Sage, for example, is a bush. It needs a pretty big pot. Oregano also grows rather large, and needs a large container. Although technically a fruit, tomatoes are probably the most popular "vegetable" for home gardeners in general.

Container gardeners are no exception, and they plant tomatoes in droves. It's probably due mostly to the fact that good tomatoes can be very difficult to find. The tomatoes in most grocery stores are picked green and artificially ripened so they survive shipping without bruising and last longer on the shelves.

Most tomato varieties can be grown very well in containers, especially cherry tomatoes, grape tomatoes, roma tomatoes, and small salad tomatoes. Other plants that are commonly grown in containers include lettuce and other salad greens, cucumbers, squashes, many types of beans and peas, radishes, carrots, scallions, all types of peppers, and even corn and potatoes.

Most vegetables can be grown in containers if you use the proper procedure. You can easily grow most of your plants from seeds. If you're growing plants indoors, you can sow directly into the pot if you like, but you can risk damaging delicate seedlings during thinning.

You should probably grow most of your plants from seedlings that you purchase locally, but you can also start your own seedlings indoors in smaller pots, and then transplant them into larger pots later. It's easier to start plants from seedlings when you can, but you may find a lot of satisfaction in starting your own.

**Locating an Outdoor Container Victory Garden**

Choosing a good location for your outdoor container garden is essential. If you choose the wrong location, it could mean disaster for your plants. The right location is one in which the plants get just the right amount of sun, are protected from harm from various outside influences, and is in a convenient spot for you to care for the garden.

The most important part of choosing a location for your container garden is choosing a place where the amount of sunlight is correct for your plants. This may mean locating part of your garden in one area of your yard, and part of your garden in another area.

If you have several plants that require a lot of sun, and several that require shade, you'll either have to split your garden into two sections, or you'll have to provide shade to those plants that need it.

This can be relatively simple for a container garden. If you just have a few plants that require shade, you can set up some sort of shade system. Using a tarp or other shade system, you can fashion a frame over your plants that blocks sun for most of the day, depending on how much shade the plants need. This way, you can locate your shade-loving plants with your sun-loving plants.

Next, you need to be sure to keep your plants away from the street, if possible. Pollution from vehicles on the road might damage your plants. Cars can also kick up dust that could settle on your plants, and their tires can also potentially throw rocks and other debris that could damage plants or break pots.

You should also try to keep your container garden as close to your house as possible. There are several reasons why you want to do this. First of all, you need to be able to easily reach your garden to take care of it. If you locate the garden too far from your house, you may be hesitant to tend to it.

Also, the closer to your house your garden is located, the less likely it is that it will be harmed by critters. Rabbits, deer, gophers, and other garden pests don't like to get too close to human scent. If you keep your garden closer to your home, the animals will be able to smell your scent more strongly and might be unwilling to approach your garden.

Another great reason for locating your garden near your home is in case you need to move your plants indoors. Sometimes you might have unexpected bad weather or other problems, and you might find a need to bring your plants inside to protect them. If the plants are closer to your house, they'll be easier to bring in.

If you have had a garden in a particular location in the past few years, and it had heavy infestation from insects, you might consider putting your garden in another part of your yard. Sometimes pests will return the following year to a previous location in search of the same food they had the year before. If you relocate your garden, you have a small chance of keeping these insects from finding your garden this year.

If you're growing very large plants like corn, choosing the right location from the start is extremely important. These large plants may be too heavy or too awkward to move safely, so they must be located correctly from the beginning. Careful planning can avoid any location disasters, so be careful to plan your garden thoroughly.

## 22. Edible Landscapes For Survivalist

Many people are choosing to move to creating more natural landscapes, even landscapes which contain plants that are useful, or can be eaten. Many vegetable plants are very attractive, and a lot of edible plants have ornamental varieties.

Most people who create edible landscapes use perennial vegetables, because they come back year after year, without the need to replant them each year. Once you've planted them, they'll continue to provide you with beauty and food as long as you care for them.

A little watering and feeding is all most of them need, aside from the occasional weeding, pruning, or insect control. There are plenty of varieties of vegetables that you can plant that will keep feeding you year after year.

They'll usually die during the winter, but every spring they'll return and go through a growth cycle again. With the prices of fresh vegetables and fruits rising at an alarming rate, it's a very good idea to grow some of your own.

You might not want the responsibility of caring for a traditional garden. Traditional gardens require a lot of work to maintain. You must constantly weed, rake, hoe, water, fertilize, and spray traditional gardens. But edible landscapes require little more effort than traditional landscapes!

You can use many different types of edible plants to replace various aspects of traditional landscaping. You can use fruit trees in place of standard trees. Many perennial herbs can be used to replace ground covers and shrubs. And ornamental vegetables can be used in place of flowers, borders, or other accents.

You can also mix edible plants with other plants to form beautiful combinations. Some edible plants, especially herbs, make great additions to flower gardens. You can mix all kinds of plants together for different looks.

Curly parsley looks beautiful with many different types of plants. You can plant it with pansies, lobelia, strawberries, dusty miller, or dianthus. Sage and oregano are very beautiful plants, and make great low shrubbery. They look fantastic as edging in front of larger bushes.

Leaf lettuces look lovely planted in beds as accent areas. You can plant a bed of different colors and varieties of leaf lettuce, and then edge it with a border grass. There are several types of plants that have edible flowers.

Many of these plants also have other edible parts. They can look very striking as part of a landscape while they're in bloom. Sugar snap peas have gorgeous white, pink, or purple flowers, and they produce delicious peas.

Fava beans produce white and red flowers. Chives have amazing purple globe-shaped flowers. Dill has lovely yellowish blossoms. Nasturtium blossoms are edible, and some in red, yellow, and orange. Sage has blue and purple blossoms. And salvia also has blue and purple blooms.

Perennial herbs and vegetables are superb for planting in edible landscapes, because they require so little maintenance. You can try perennial broccoli, dandelions, sweet potatoes, rhubarb, sorrel, artichokes and Jerusalem artichokes, chives, fennel, garlic chives, ginger, and asparagus.

**Planning Your Edible Landscape**

Edible landscaping is the process of planting edible plants in a landscape, rather than in a traditional garden. There are two major benefits to edible landscaping. First of all, edible landscapes save space, because they combine landscaping and food-growing into a single space.

Secondly, they turn a standard landscape into more than just aesthetics, but into a useful method of growing some of your own food. Edible landscapes don't have to be 100% edible. You can design your edible landscape around any percentage of edible plants you wish.

You might choose to make your landscape 100% edible, or you might only include a single fruit tree. Edible landscaping has actually been around for a very long time. Some of the earliest edible landscapes were found in ancient Persia and in gardens in medieval times.

In some areas of the world, most people plant mostly edible varieties. Some people see no point in planting anything that isn't edible, seeing everything else as a waste of valuable food-growing space.

An important part of planning your edible landscape is knowing what conditions each variety needs. Some plants will need a lot of sun, and some plants require more shade. You need to be sure the soil conditions are suitable.

Be sure to check each and every variety so you know its soil requirements, sunlight requirements, and the nutrient and pH balance needed. Start by planning out your landscape on paper.

Mark off where you want to place certain plants, and be sure those areas are conducive to the varieties you wish to locate there. Use fruit trees in place of shade trees. You can plant hazelnuts and currants wherever you might place a deciduous shrub. You can use herbs in place of low-lying shrubs and ground cover.

Ornamental plants often need very little care. Edible plants do need a little bit more attention than other plants if you want them to produce a good harvest. You might have to water them more often or fertilizer them.

You'll probably have to work a bit harder to control pests than you would for strictly ornamental plants, because insects tend to target edible plants much more often. But the food yield certainly makes it worth a bit of additional work.

One of the most important types of edible plants to add to a landscape is fruit trees or bushes. Fruit trees make excellent shade tree replacements. And berry bushes can be extremely attractive in place of typical shrubs. Blueberry bushes can be quite lovely in front of a home, for example. And apple trees can grow into delightful shade trees!

Instead of planting flowerbeds, you can plant beds of lettuce, herbs, or greens. Many types of mint have lovely blooms. Lettuce and other greens can come in all types of colors. You can get ornamental cabbages and kale in a wide variety of colors, adding a splash of color to any area. Peppers and tomatoes are colorful additions, as well.

Grape arbors are a spectacular addition to a landscape. Grape arbors have been used for many years as a beautiful enhancement to lawns, and the fruit is a wonderful bonus. Remember, many types of flowers are also edible.

Nasturtiums, violas, daylilies, calendula, and borage are all edible, and make wonderful additions to salads and decorations for cakes. So you can still plant some flowers, even if you want to stay 100% edible!

**Using Perennial Vegetables for Landscaping**

Planting perennial vegetables as part of your landscape is a great idea, because it helps you make maximum use of your space. Instead of hurting your beautiful landscape by tearing up your lawn to plant a traditional garden, you can simply work your food plants into your existing landscape.

You can use a wide variety of perennial vegetables and herbs as part of your landscape, and they can be just as beautiful as traditional landscape plants. Perennial vegetables are great, because you don't have to replant them each year.

You plant them once, and with a small amount of ongoing maintenance, you'll have a beautiful landscape and fresh food every year. Perennials need to be planted in good conditions right from the start.

If you plant annuals in poor soil or a bad location, you've only lost a single year. But if you plant perennials improperly, you've wasted a plant that could have grown for many years.
First of all, be sure you plant your perennials in a good location right from the start.

Check the required growing conditions for the variety before you plant it. Make sure you choose a spot that has the proper amount of sunlight for the plant. Don't forget to take into account the potential growth of any other nearby plants! If you plant something in a sunny location, it might be shady in a year or two if surrounding plants grow larger.

Be sure to prepare your soil before planting. It's much easier to modify the soil before planting than it is to make corrections later. Be sure the soil has the proper pH levels and nutrient levels, and make certain your soil will support the correct moisture level for the plants. You'll need to be certain to have the right balance, because different plant varieties require different types of soil.

Another thing to keep in mind is your zone. Some perennial plants won't be very tolerant of extreme heat or frosts, so care in this matter is essential. The point of planting perennials is to have plants that return each year. If they die completely in the winter, they won't return in the spring, so be sure you get your zone correct.

There are many perennial herbs that make a great addition to an edible landscape. Many types of mint are perennial in a lot of zones. They have beautiful foliage, and some of them have very pretty blossoms. Other perennial herbs that are ideal for landscaping include French tarragon, lavender, chives, Greek oregano, English Thyme, garlic chives, lemon balm, and sage.

A lot of vegetables are quite attractive, and can be very nice in landscapes. Perennial varieties of chard, beans, and broccoli are all great for landscapes. Asparagus, sorrel, fennel, ginger, artichokes, Jerusalem artichokes, chicory, sweet potatoes, rhubarb, rocket, and sorrel are all great choices.

You can also use other edible plants for your landscaping. Fruit trees are an obvious choice. Many fruit trees have absolutely stunning blooms. Cherry trees, apple trees, and plum trees all have lovely blooms that will make a great addition to your landscape. The fruits they bear can also add an amazing color and style to your yard. Having bright red cherries and golden apples can really enhance a landscape.

**Great Plants for Edible Landscapes**

There are hundreds of edible plants that would look perfectly lovely in a landscape, but some of them work better than others. Many plants won't look very good later in the season, for example.

Some of them quickly turn dark and lose their leaves. You want plants that taste great, but keep their appearance long enough to be a practical part of your landscape. It's no good to build plants that lose their looks in late summer into your landscape design!

Here's a look at some of the best choices for edible plants for landscape design. We'll mostly be including plants that require minimal care and look attractive, while providing something very edible:

- 'Golden Streaks' is a variety of mustard that has heavily serrated leaves in a beautiful golden citron color. It has a very mild taste, slightly sweet. This is a striking plant that has a wonderful flavor.

- 'Hansel Hybrid' eggplant is a stunning plant. It has a two-foot-tall plant that produces huge clusters of fingerling eggplants in a delightful deep purple hue.

- 'Pesto Perpetuo' basil is a one to two foot basil plant with absolutely gorgeous variegated leaves. The leaves are a rich green with a fringe of white. It tastes like Greek basil, but the appearance is wonderful in a landscape!

- 'Purple Peacock' broccoli is a hybrid cross between broccoli and two different types of kale. It has a purple stem and loose, purple head.

- 'Violetta Hybrid' pak choi is an amazing variety of this Chinese green. It has lovely purple leaves that are packed with more nutrients than many other types of greens!

- 'Red Popper' is a type of miniature bell pepper. The fruits are only about one to two inches in diameter and are very sweet and delicious. You'll love the way these bright red peppers look against the rich, green foliage!

- 'Sweet Lace' grapes are a small, patio-sized variety of grape. They have very pretty leaves and produce pretty white grapes in September. These can be grown in containers, and they can also be trellised easily. They make a beautiful accent to a fence or wall.

- 'Red Veined' sorrel is a variety of this classic wild green. It has light green leaves with a truly spectacular series of red veins all throughout. The taste is very sharp, so it's best in salads with mild greens. This one is particularly striking in appearance.

- 'Purple Mizuna' is a fabulous type of greens. They have a very tangy flavor, and grow very quickly. Mizuna greens are already quite attractive, but this purple variety is particularly nice.

- 'Mittistone' is a summer-crisp lettuce of the loose-leaf variety. The leaves are green with red speckles. It is a sweet, crisp lettuce variety that tastes as amazing as it looks. It matures quickly, and looks just as beautiful in your yard as it does in a salad bowl.

## Edible Flowers in Edible Landscapes

Most people grow flowers strictly for their aesthetic value. Not many people realize that there are a lot of flower varieties that can be eaten. Flowers can bring amazing flavor and color to salads, and make stunning decorations for cakes and other dishes.

Flowers can also be used to make teas, and their flavor extracts can be used in cakes, frostings, candies, and other foods. Many flowers are also very good for you. Roses are very high in vitamin C, especially rose hips.

Nasturtiums and marigolds also have a decent amount of vitamin C, and dandelion flowers contain both vitamin C and vitamin A. If a flower isn't poisonous, it's considered technically edible, but not all edible flowers are tasty.

Just keep in mind that you should be absolutely certain what you're eating, because some flowers have poisonous look-alikes! You should never eat flowers if you have hay fever, asthma, or other allergies.

Never eat flowers that have been sprayed with any type of pesticide. And be sure to choose only blossoms that haven't wilted. Remember, even edible flowers should be eaten in moderate amounts.

Some people may still have minor reactions to large amounts of edible flowers. Some common flowering plants should NEVER be eaten. Lily-of-the-valley is highly toxic, for example. Other flowers that shouldn't be eaten include hydrangeas, azaleas, daffodils, wisteria, lupines, hyacinths, castor beans, rhododendrons, sweet peas, clematis, bleeding hearts, oleander, and calla lilies.

This is just a partial list! Always carefully research any flower before eating it, and even check varieties of the same type of flower. For landscaping purposes, you should probably concentrate on perennials.

Now let's look at some of the very best blooming plants and flowers for landscaping. Remember, these are all perennials, since our purpose is creating landscaping:

- Dianthus comes in shades of red, white, and pink. It tastes similar to cloves.
- Daylilies come in many colors and taste a bit like squash or asparagus.

- Red clover has pink or red flowers that taste delicate and sweet.
- Tulips are mild and sweet and come in many different colors.
- Violets are slightly sweet, slightly sour. They come in pink, white, purple, and blue.
- Chives have beautiful pink globes of blossoms that taste very much like onions.
- Bee balm has pink, red, white, and lavender flowers that taste a bit like tea.
- Hollyhocks are slightly bitter and come in many colors.
- Borage tastes a lot like cucumbers, and comes in blue, purple, and lavender.

Perennials will continue to come back year after year, without the need for replanting each year. This is a very important part of landscaping, since landscaping should require only minimal maintenance.

# 23. Permaculture – Path To Long Term Sustainability & Survival

We live in an increasingly industrially reliant culture. A culture that relies on fast food, disposable goods and cheap gasoline. A culture that is fast eating itself up. Enter Permaculture.

Permaculture is another way to look at the world and its resources. We'll look at just what is meant by permaculture, the history of this conservation movement and meet some of its originators and the future of Permaculture. You may find that you are already applying some of the basic tenants of this small but growing movement.

Permaculture, as you may have guessed, is a contraction of the words permanent culture. The idea being that we rely more on sustainable agriculture not dependent on fossil fuels.

It will use local resources, smaller more diverse crop planning, non-chemically dependent fertilizing, for example. Permaculture is a movement away from anything big and industrial to the smaller and sustainable farms, encouraging more interdependence with community members.

It all began in the '70s by a wildlife biologist and ecologist named Bill Mollison of Australia. He saw the growing monster of the Industrial revolution and its impact on our culture.

How this kind of culture was bound to eventually cave in due to its monstrous appetite. Rather than reacting in a negative way to this, he instead decided to take a more positive approach.

By studying nature, he came to several conclusions about how nature goes through sustainable cycles without the benefit of man. Bill began to live and then to teach his philosophy.

Another man who has silently built up a following in this movement is Masanobu Fukuoka. He believes that you should disturb the soil to an absolute minimum. Seeds are planted right on the soil's surface and then lightly covered with straw or other light mulch.

Weeds are trimmed before the flower stage and allowed to become part of the mulch. This kills unwanted vegetation without poison and gives a favorable soil in which to plant. In time the soil becomes healthy and weeds and pests become less of a concern.

Ruth Stout is another voice in this community. Her ideas about "no-till" gardening have caused many to change their views about weeds and weeding. Similar to Fukuoka, she purported to never need to weed but allowed plants to grow together.

All vegetation, both "good" and "bad," build the soil which leads to healthy crops which means fewer pests. Once the soil is built weeding becomes as simple as flicking out the weed. All without chemicals and pesticides.

From its small, quiet revolutionary beginnings, it is apparent that permaculture will have to be embraced to a greater or lesser degree. Pollution due to industrial waste and mass transportation systems are on their way down memory lane. It will cost too much to ship in food from across the country so it makes more and more sense to buy food grown locally or grow it yourself.

Permaculture as a basic philosophy has grown and spread its less intrusive approach to living on and using the earth. While nowadays it seems to be associated with second and third generation "hippies," even Urbanites practice it by growing a garden for vegetables and tossing the trimmings back on the beds. Yes, permaculture, In all its varied philosophies will impact our lives - for the good.

**The Core Concepts of Permaculture Design**

To understand any subject that's new to us, it helps to dig into its key concepts. Understanding permaculture at its basic sense will help people to perhaps see how some of its elements can be applied in their own life.

Specifically, we will deal with, sustainability, minimal disruption of soil conditions, and interdependence with our neighbors. Let's begin by talking about how permaculture contributes to sustainability of the earth's ecosystems.

It isn't by accident that permanent is part of the term permaculture. Here we have a way to work with the way nature works not in a forced, mechanized way of modern times. When you use hand tools and human labor, you don't need to depend on the fossil fuels.

Naturally built up soils don't support disease and pests so you don't need petroleum-based pesticides and fertilizers. When you don't remove the unused part of the plant but just lay it back down on the soil to mulch you reduce labor and eliminate the need to amend the soil. Mulching aids water retention and thus reduces need to water.

The ultimate in sustainability is when end of year harvest comes, you allow several plants to go to seed. Then you can cut down the dying foliage and seed heads and lay this on the ground with the mulch which will go on to seed for next year's crops. This like the other core concepts is the hallmark of permaculture - giving back to the land everything but the fruits you consume.

Another core concept of permaculture is the idea of soil conservation and minimally disturbing the soils in which we plant. Permaculturists will use hand tools rather than tillers and tractors, which does several things to harm the soil. Heavier equipment compacts the soil, which makes the ground more difficult to use.

It is a fact that intensive gardening increases crop production 10 fold when soil is not compacted and soil is left loose and friable. This way we can get 10 times more production out of the same amount of land - which translates to 10 times more food available to feed the population of the world. No more food shortages. It may be hard to believe that we can get more production out of less land by eliminating machinery, but permaculture has proved this time and again.

A final key concept of permaculture is rebuilding community. Because of our industrialized society we have become detached from each other not just as family but also as community.

This causes us to turn to government and corporations to fill our needs, which causes lower quality food because of the need for mass production, as well as diminishing the local job base, and creating more of a need for outside energy input.

If you buy raw milk from the diary down the road, beef from your neighbor and vegetables from the local organic farmer, you not only provide work for them, you also get higher quality food, with less fossil fuel input. This creates a sustainable loop of profitable work, quality products that we actually need, and utilizes local sources.

In an increasing global economy suffering from constant disruptions in the job market and food chain, this is the future we must work toward for our children and grandchildren. To create a "permanent" culture, we must strive for sustainability, minimal disruption of the soil, and interdependence and shared resources.

## How to Grow a Permaculture Garden

While we may not be able to make large changes, a whole lot of little changes can add up to a revolution. A small way to make a big change is to grow a garden using permaculture techniques.

What makes a garden a small permaculture? You can learn about garden preparation tools and techniques, how to plant and tend to a garden that is raised sustainably. It takes far less time to garden in this way than you may think.

The idea behind permaculture gardening is to use only hand tools and minimal human labor. The only tools you'll need are a shovel, rake and small trowel. The idea here is to not disturb the soil any more than necessary.

Tilling the soil will introduce too much oxygen, which acts to kill the soil organisms that live on and around plant roots. This allows for weeds, which are less "picky" about the soil in which they grow.

Plot preparation can be as simple as layering a mat of cardboard or thick layers of newsprint where you plan to plant. If the weeds are well established, cut them down before you layer the cardboard.

There's no concern here about existing vegetation as the thick cardboard mulch will kill the weeds. So, we have eliminated dubious chemicals and poisons from your garden shed.

On top of this you will layer 6 to 12 inches of straw laid out in rows so you can walk between hills. Here the idea is to keep the rows no wider than you can comfortably reach from both sides. Notice we didn't till, dig or poison the garden plot. It is so much simpler to use permaculture techniques in your garden.

To plant seeds, you can sprinkle them right on the soil's surface in most cases. Then pull any mulch over this. The mulch acts to help the soil retain moisture so you don't have to water as often. The mulch gradually breaks down and adds to the soil, as the seeds germinate and grow.

Planting starts like lettuce is easy as pulling back the straw, poking a hole in the cardboard, placing the little plant in and pushing back the straw. This works even in heavy soils. Allow the greenery of the plant starts to barely come above the mulch, even gently pulling off an older leaf to stimulate growth.

When it comes to weeding, it is a simple matter of snipping the emerging greenery and leaving it to add to the mulch. The idea is to not let the weeds go to the flowering stage where they would quickly go to seed.

At time of harvest, you take a head of lettuce, for example, and would just cut the head off and leave the roots. The lettuce will continue to produce some leaves till the first frost that you may continue to harvest and use.

Over winter the roots will die and add to the soil. When harvesting beans or tomatoes, you take the fruit; pull the greens and leave to break down with the mulch. No composting this way and no waste.

Learning permaculture is possibly one of the most responsible skills any homeowner and gardener could learn and as you can see it isn't like learning rocket science. Take a strong back and a rake to the garden next spring.

Printed in Great Britain
by Amazon